READING MICHAEL CHABON

Recent Titles in
The Pop Lit Book Club

READING MICHAEL CHABON

Helene Meyers

The Pop Lit Book Club

GREENWOOD

AN IMPRINT OF ABC-CLIO, LLC
Santa Barbara, California • Denver, Colorado • Oxford, England

813.09
CHABON, M
MEYERS, H

Library of Congress Cataloging-in-Publication Data

Meyers, Helene.
  Reading Michael Chabon / Helene Meyers.
    p. cm. — (The pop lit book club)
  Includes bibliographical references and index.
  ISBN 978-0-313-35550-9 (hard copy : acid-free paper)—ISBN 978-0-313-35551-6 (ebook)
  1. Chabon, Michael—Criticism and interpretation. I. Title.
  PS3553.H15Z77 2010
  813'.54—dc22   2009052853

ISBN: 978-0-313-35550-9
EISBN: 978-0-313-35551-6

14   13   12   11   10   1   2   3   4   5

This book is also available on the World Wide Web as an eBook.
Visit www.abc-clio.com for details.

Greenwood
An Imprint of ABC-CLIO, LLC

ABC-CLIO, LLC
130 Cremona Drive, P.O. Box 1911
Santa Barbara, California 93116-1911

This book is printed on acid-free paper ∞

Manufactured in the United States of America

CONTENTS

PREFACE

Reading Michael Chabon is the first book-length volume devoted to the works of a writer who bridges the gap between literary and popular culture and whose novels lend themselves to film adaptations. Designed for book club members and students (both high school and college), this reference guide will help readers keep track of Chabon's intricate plots, draw thematic connections between his major novels, and understand his fiction as cultural commentary on contemporary masculinity and Jewish identity. The information, analysis, and discussion questions provided here should initiate lively conversation and debate about an author who not only writes about wonder boys but has become one himself.

Since writers' lives help to shape but do not determine their creative choices, *Reading Michael Chabon* (like all volumes in The Pop Lit Book Club series) begins with a biographical sketch. In this first chapter, the reader will find a brief overview of this Pulitzer Prize–winning author's literary career. Since Chabon's major works are novels, the next chapter discusses his contributions to that genre, with particular attention to coming-of-age narratives, the picaresque, detective fiction, and the Jewish American novel. Each of the following four chapters focuses on one of his major novels to date: *The Mysteries of Pittsburgh*, *Wonder Boys*, *The Amazing Adventures of Kavalier and Clay*, and *The Yiddish Policemen's Union*. In these chapters, readers will find a summary of the narrative, an annotated list of characters, and a discussion of major themes.

Subsequent chapters discuss Chabon in relation to contemporary culture. Intense male-male relationships are a constant in his fiction, and his work has become increasingly and explicitly Jewish-centered. These overlapping issues form the core of one of these chapters while Chabon's embrace of popular culture is the subject of another chapter—in particular, the completed and anticipated film adaptations of his novels, his love affair with comics, and his forays into detective and adventure fiction. From fan sites to YouTube, Chabon has an impressive presence on the Internet; thus, the chapter "Michael Chabon on the Internet" includes some sites and guidance for those who seek to surf the Web for more information and who want to understand the role that the Internet plays in promoting literary culture and community.

Michael Chabon's novels are widely reviewed, and interviews with him have been broadcast on National Public Radio (NPR) and have appeared in major newspapers. Chabon has even appeared on an episode of *The Simpsons*. The chapter "Michael Chabon and the Media" provides an overview of critical response to Chabon's work as well as his use of diverse media.

Reading Michael Chabon concludes with two chapters which provide suggestions for further study by book club members and students. Those who appreciate Chabon's fiction will want to consult the recommended reading list in "What Do I Read Next?" to discover comparable and complementary works by other writers. The final section, "Resources," is a bibliography of print and electronic sources that all readers can consult for further information and that students can use for research assignments.

Readers who have particular interests should make use of the index to find all relevant information. For instance, the index entry for *The Mysteries of Pittsburgh* points the book club participant or the student writing an essay not only to the chapter devoted solely to that novel but also to relevant sections of other chapters (e.g., the discussion of *Mysteries* as a coming-of-age novel in Chapter 2 and media commentary on Chabon's first novel in Chapter 10). Similarly, the index identifies pertinent material across chapters for those wanting to know more about a specific topic such as the Holocaust in Chabon's fiction or his depiction of gay characters and relationships.

ACKNOWLEDGMENTS

Although the actual writing of a book is a solitary endeavor, conversations and encouragement make those hours in front of a computer screen not only possible but also pleasurable. I'm profoundly grateful to George Butler for inviting me to write this volume for Greenwood and to Guy P. Raffa and Jean Kane for encouraging me to accept that invitation. The participants in the Austin Nextbook/ALA book series on Jewish literature as well as students who have taken my Contemporary Jewish Literature courses in recent years motivated me to write for a general audience. Brooke Arnold provided invaluable research assistance; I look forward to the books and articles that she will soon be writing.

Staff members at Southwestern University's Smith Library Center are exemplary in their commitment to scholar-teachers; in particular, I want to thank Dana Hendrix, Carol Fonken, and Lisa Anderson. Alan Berger, Alisa Braun, and Ranen Omer-Sherman participated in a roundtable on Michael Chabon's work that I organized; I learned much from their insightful commentary. Other colleagues whose intellectual energy has, in one way or another, contributed to this volume include Eileen Cleere, Jim Kilfoyle, Lisa Moses Leff, John Pipkin, and Elizabeth Stockton. I am grateful for financial support from both the Cullen Faculty Development Fund and the McManis University Chair Research Fund.

As always, my deepest gratitude, respect, and affection go to the inimitable Susan Gubar. Del Garcia, Connie Haham, Lea Isgur, Sandi Simon, and Monica Solomon always evince interest in my work; I thank them for the happy hours that I often spend with them on Saturday mornings. My father, the late Alfred Meyers, would have been jazzed by this book; as I have matured, so has my appreciation of his hard-boiled integrity. I consider myself blessed to share the values of menschlikhkeit with my partner, Guy; the pleasures of writing this book have been greatly enhanced by his love, patience, counsel, and cooking.

MICHAEL CHABON: A WRITER'S LIFE

In a review of *Wonder Boys*, Jonathan Yardley proclaimed Michael Chabon "the young star of American letters, 'star' not in the current sense of cheap celebrity but in the old one of brightly shining hope." Erik Spanberg has deemed Chabon the "coolest writer in America." *Esquire* recently included him in its list of "the 75 most influential people of the 21st century." Nora Ephron, writing for *O, the Oprah Magazine*, detailed the rapture of reading Chabon's Pulitzer Prize–winning novel *The Amazing Adventures of Kavalier and Clay*. Such diverse accolades point to the dual nature of his writing career: considered one of the major literary voices of his generation, he is also immensely popular. Chabon's novels have regularly appeared on the *New York Times* Best Sellers List. His first two novels—*The Mysteries of Pittsburgh* and *Wonder Boys*—already have been adapted into films, and the film rights to both *Kavalier and Clay* and *The Yiddish Policemen's Union* have been acquired. Chabon has produced major American novels and successfully linked contemporary American letters to genre fiction not only with those novels but also with *The Final Solution: A Story of Detection*, a detective novella; *Gentlemen of the Road*, an adventure narrative; and *Summerland*, a young adult fantasy novel. Refusing to choose between literary quality and entertainment, Chabon resides on the borderlands of popular culture and high art.

Chabon's upbringing in Columbia, Maryland, set the stage for a creative life that resists prefabricated limits. In 1969, when he was six, his parents decided to participate in a social experiment: the building of a visionary, interracial community. He remembers the Exhibit Center of Columbia that contained a map with names of villages and neighborhoods, many of which had not yet been built. Thus, he learned the power of words and the imagination to conjure place. As he watched houses "being born" and played in areas beyond "the edge of the Known World," he found the model for a writing career in which he ventures off into "terra incognita" (Chabon, "Maps and Legends," *Maps and Legends*, 32–33). However, his youth in Columbia also taught him about loss and disillusionment as his parents, Robert and Sharon, divorced, and racial tensions and crime infiltrated Columbia.

Michael Chabon wrote his first short story as a preteen; titled "The Revenge of Nemo," it chronicled the meeting of Sherlock Holmes and Captain Nemo, with Dr. Watson as the voice of the piece. Praised for this juvenilia, Chabon realized that writing might be his life's work. He was also an avid reader of comic books, which functioned as a sort of paternal inheritance. His grandfather was a printer at a plant that produced comics, so he used to bring them home for Chabon's father. Chabon's dad continued this tradition and brought Michael comics "by the bagful" (Conan). Although he found himself particularly enamored with the origins and exploits of superheroes, he was addicted to all genres of comics with the exception of true romance.

Chabon earned his undergraduate degree in English from the University of Pittsburgh. In the summer between graduating college and beginning an MFA in creative writing at the University of California, Irvine, he found himself worrying that all of his future classmates were novelists. Moreover, living in Oakland that summer with his mother, he longed for his life in Pittsburgh. Influenced by his reading of F. Scott Fitzgerald's *The Great Gatsby* and Philip Roth's *Goodbye, Columbus*, he installed himself in his mother's basement and began writing what became his master's thesis and his first novel, *The Mysteries of Pittsburgh*. Unbeknownst to Chabon, one of his writing professors at Irvine, Donald Heiney, sent *The Mysteries of Pittsburgh* manuscript to his own agent. As a result, nine publishers competed for it, and Chabon was awarded an unprecedented advance of $155,000 for a first novel from William Morrow. He was 24 when that novel was published.

His status as literary wonder boy and his boyish good looks provided him with opportunities for other kinds of celebrity, which he resisted. He was courted to do an advertisement for GAP jeans and refused; likewise, he abstained from becoming one of *People* magazine's "50 most beautiful people." However, he did accept an advance contract for his next novel and found himself floundering as he struggled to complete

Fountain City. He spent more than five years on this ill-fated 1,500-page manuscript; even after he edited it down to 700 pages, it still was not worthy of publication. Chabon confesses that he could never really define what *Fountain City* was about: characters included an Israeli spy, an AIDS patient, and an architect working on plans for a perfect ball-park; the dual settings of Paris and Fountain City were at odds, and a plot to build anew the Temple in Jerusalem further complicated this mess of a novel. Although *Fountain City* never came into being, Chabon speculates that "it'll be like this incredible shipwreck that I'll be feeding off of, like Robinson Crusoe, for the next 30 years" (Giles). The fact that a plan to rebuild the Temple figures prominently in *The Yiddish Policemen's Union* and that baseball and its mythic fields are central to *Summerland* suggests the wisdom of Chabon's philosophic attitude toward this failed novel.

Chabon's marriage to writer Lollie Groth did not survive the mete-oric rise of his career with *The Mysteries of Pittsburgh* and his subse-quent flailing on *Fountain City*. They divorced in 1991. He met his current wife, lawyer-cum-writer Ayelet Waldman, on a blind date; she proposed to him three weeks later. During the six weeks that she inten-sively studied for her bar exam, Chabon gave himself permission to put *Fountain City* on hold and to follow the vision he had of a young man holding a gun to his head and a "shaggy old watcher in the shadows" (Chabon, "Diving into the Wreck," *Maps and Legends*, 160). Thus, Cha-bon began *Wonder Boys* and transformed his trauma of writing and rewriting *Fountain City* into the sometimes poignant, sometimes uproar-ious adventures of Grady Tripp, a creative writing professor who can't seem to stop writing a novel that has already exceeded 2,000 pages. Chabon readily admits that Tripp was a "projection of my worst fears of what I was going to become if I kept working on *Fountain City*" (See). In writing the foibles of Tripp and exorcising his own writerly demons, Chabon rediscovered the fluid composing process that he had experi-enced while working on *The Mysteries of Pittsburgh*.

Although Michael Chabon was gratified by Jonathan Yardley's praise of *Wonder Boys* and its star-like author, he ultimately agreed with Yard-ley's assessment that he needed to move beyond the limited scope of both *The Mysteries of Pittsburgh* and *Wonder Boys* to realize his full potential as a writer. Chabon had been looking for an opportunity to set a novel in the New York of his father's childhood. Sitting in a dentist's office, he read a *Smithsonian* article about Superman's creators Jerry Siegel and Joe Shuster which caused Chabon to reflect on the link that the Golden Age of comics had forged between his father's childhood and his own. This became the genesis for *The Amazing Adventures of*

Kavalier and Clay, a work whose historic span and transatlantic settings signaled a new level of literary ambition. The research for *Kavalier and Clay* included immersion in comic book history as well as the culture and trivia of New York of the pre- and post–World War II period. Chabon also interviewed such towering figures as Will Eisner, creator of *The Spirit*, and he visited Prague. In *Kavalier and Clay*, he used the Jewish legend of the golem, a man of clay brought to life through the power of words, as an antecedent to the superheroes created by so many Jewish American comic book artists. The golem begins as a protector of Jews but ends up as a destructive force, often evading the control of and even damaging his creator. For Chabon, the risks of golem-making parallel and symbolize the risks of writing, in particular the self-exposure that results whether or not one writes autobiographically.

Described by Ken Kalfus in the *New York Times* as a "novel of towering achievement," *Kavalier and Clay* was nominated for both the National Book Critics Circle Award and the PEN/Faulkner Award but won neither. Thus, Michael Chabon was astonished when his wife Ayelet, eight months pregnant with their third child, answered the phone one afternoon and leaped into his arms as she delivered the news that he had won the Pulitzer Prize for *The Amazing Adventures of Kavalier and Clay*.

In 2002, Chabon published *Summerland*, a young adult fantasy novel dedicated to his children Sophie, Zeke, and Ida-Rose (his fourth child, Abraham, had not yet been born). This novel represents Chabon's lifetime infatuation with baseball. Chabon's father was a Brooklyn Dodgers fan and thus had his heart broken when the Dodgers moved to Los Angeles. Chabon experienced the betrayal of his own first boyhood baseball love when the Washington Senators left the D.C. area and became the Texas Rangers. He then became a fan of the Pittsburgh Pirates, only to be devastated by the tragic, untimely death of Roberto Clemente. The ritual of reading aloud to his children at bedtime as well as his sense that baseball books for young readers did not convey the sport as American mythology inspired this novel about baseball as a vehicle for saving the universe. The hero of the story, Ethan Feld, is not a baseball enthusiast, whereas his close friend, Jennifer T. Rideout, is quite the fan and player. Chabon credits his daughter Sophie for his invention of Jennifer, since Sophie is "extremely prejudiced against fiction that doesn't have strong female characters" and "hates books where the girl is just being rescued over and over again" (Miller). *Summerland* appeared on the *New York Times* Children's Literature Bestseller List; just as importantly, Chabon's sentence "A baseball game is nothing but a great contraption to get you to pay attention to the cadence of a summer afternoon" earned the unsolicited comment of "nice" from Sophie (Miller).

Chabon's admiration for Sir Arthur Conan Doyle, the creator of Sherlock Holmes, is manifest not only in his juvenilia but in his 2004 novella *The Final Solution: A Story of Detection*. This novella, which first appeared in print in the *Paris Review*, features an aged and unnamed Holmes. Chabon's title alludes to "The Final Problem," the Conan Doyle fictional story in which Holmes seemingly dies, as well as to Hitler's and Nazi Germany's very real genocidal plot against the Jews. *The Final Solution* garnered a National Jewish Book Award, besting Cynthia Ozick's *Heir to the Glimmering World* and Philip Roth's *The Plot Against America*.

Chabon's 2007 novel *The Yiddish Policemen's Union* began with an essay that he wrote for *Civilization* after returning to the States from his first trip to Israel and finding a copy of Uriel and Beatrice Weinreich's 1958 phrasebook, *Say It in Yiddish*. Unaware of the vast community of Yiddish-speaking survivors in Israel as well as of Uriel Weinreich as an eminent scholar of Yiddish who died quite young, Chabon initially viewed this phrasebook as a "heartbreakingly implausible book" and ruefully imagined a world in which "Yiddish would not be, as it is in ours, a tin can with no tin can on the other end of the string" (Chabon, "Imaginary Homelands," *Maps and Legends*, 177, 180). Chabon's uncle, Stanley Werbow, informed his nephew that his essay, reprinted in *Harper's*, had outraged Yiddish scholars; indeed, a contentious discussion took place on the Internet via the academic listserv Mendele. Receiving a letter from Mrs. Weinreich that conveyed her belief that he had been disrespectful toward her late husband and Yiddish itself, Chabon responded with a letter of apology; as he explains in his essay "Imaginary Homelands," "I *felt* my ignorance and was ashamed" (186). However, he also experienced the devilish impulse that if this were the effect of "one little essay," how much greater the impact would be with "an entire *novel*" (186, 191).

To prepare for writing a novel that imagines a Jewish homeland and refuge from the Holocaust not in the Middle East but rather in Sitka, Alaska, Chabon attempted to atone for and correct his ignorance of Yiddish by using Weinreich's dictionary, "slowly, and incompletely, and painstakingly" (Brawarsky). However, in adding this body of knowledge to his novelistic repertoire, he also was returning to his youthful roots. In creating his fictional Sitka (in actuality, Sitka is an island that has a very small population of Jews), he called upon the Columbia experiment in which imagination creates a place. Says Chabon, "I was just repeating what I had seen done in the town I grew up in" (Cohen). Moreover, his maternal grandparents provided his first exposure to Yiddish; he remembers being aware that it was not only a vibrant but also a shameful "ghetto language" (Kaplan, "Politics"). Yiddish represented the lost world of his grandparents and a key to his Jewish roots. He used his mother's maiden name, Verbov, which was also the name of the Russian town from which he believes his grandmother emigrated, to identify the sect of observant Jews featured in *The Yiddish Policemen's Union*. Yet his fictional Sitka was not only an attempt to imagine a culture decimated by the Shoah but also an analogue to the Jewish homemaking he has undertaken with his Israeli-born wife, Ayelet Waldman. The first draft of *The Yiddish Policemen's Union* was 600 pages and written in the first person; Chabon regards his second draft as a "sequel" to the first (Cohen). The novel has garnered a great deal of mainstream critical attention; as an alternative history, it also has been nominated for and won two significant science fiction awards, the Hugo and the Nebula.

An alternative Jewish world also marks Chabon's *Gentlemen of the Road* (2007). This "tale of adventure" was originally published in weekly installments in the *New York Times Magazine* and reflects his wonder at discovering Khazaria. As he puts it in an interview with Julie Phillips for the *Washington Post*, "a medieval empire at war with the Vikings and Byzantium that lasted for more than four centuries, that was famous all over the world at the time, and everybody was Jewish! What? How come nobody ever told me about them?" As with *Kavalier and Clay* and *The Yiddish Policemen's Union*, Chabon first did research and then began the imaginative work of fiction. Given the limited reliable information available on the Khazars, a Turkic people, Chabon arrived at the imaginative "point a little more quickly with this book" (Siegel). Like Columbia, Maryland, and Sitka, Alaska, Chabon regarded Khazaria as "terra incognita" (Siegel). In his afterword to this short work, Chabon shares that "Jews with Swords" was the initial and "in [his] heart, true" title of this picaresque adventure.

In 2008, Chabon published his first collection of essays, *Maps and Legends: Reading and Writing along the Borderlands*. His second collection of essays, released in October 2009, is titled *Manhood for Amateurs: The Pleasures and Regrets of a Husband, Father and Son*. Many of the essays in *Manhood for Amateurs* originally appeared in the men's magazine *Details*, where Chabon has published a monthly column since October 2005. His work-in-progress is a novel of family life set in contemporary California. It features two families, one black and one white; the women are partners in midwifery, the men in business. Although Chabon is now most well-known as a novelist, early in his career he won a 1987 *Mademoiselle* short story contest for "Blumenthal in the Air," later reprinted in his collection *A Model World and Other Stories* (1991). Stories from that volume and *Werewolves in Their Youth* (1999) originally appeared in such publications as the *New Yorker*, *Harper's*, *GQ*, and *Esquire*. Chabon has edited *The Best American Short Stories* (2005) as well as *McSweeney's Enchanted Chamber of Astonishing Stories* and *McSweeney's Mammoth Treasury of Thrilling Tales*. As a screenwriter, he has worked on *Spiderman 2* and *John Carter of Mars*, a film based on the writing of Edgar Rice Burroughs which is in development. Screenwriting pays well, and as a member of the Writers Guild of America he has access to affordable health insurance for his family.

Erik Spanberg has commented that "Chabon may be a literary Superman, but he lives like Clark Kent." At home with his wife Ayelet and their four children, Chabon maintains a regular domestic and writing routine. Five days a week, he writes from 10:00 P.M. until 3:00 A.M.; he derives focus from this nocturnal solitude and the sense that he is "the only person alive in the whole world" (Wilson). Chabon developed such a disciplined writing schedule to deal with his early success. He realized that "to write your third, fourth or fifth novel" prevents the potentially corrosive effects of literary celebrity (Streitfeld, "Young Writers").

Many assumed Chabon to be a gay writer based on the relationships depicted in *The Mysteries of Pittsburgh*; even Ayelet Waldman, after reading that novel prior to their first date, wondered why she was being set up with a gay man. Waldman, the author of the *Mommy Track* mystery series as well as *Daughter's Keeper* and *Love and Other Impossible Pursuits*, created a great deal of controversy when she wrote an essay, "Truly, Madly, Guiltily," for the *New York Times* in which she asserted that she felt like a bad mother because her love for her children had not supplanted or exceeded that for her husband. In that essay, which she invokes in her memoir *Bad Mother*, she characterizes her husband as someone who takes his domestic responsibilities seriously and "loves the children the way a mother is supposed to," but certainly isn't perfect. As she puts it, "He's handsome, brilliant, and successful. But he can also be scatterbrained, antisocial, and arrogant. He is a bad dancer, and he knows far too much about Klingon politics and the lyrics to Yes songs."

The couple spends time together reading and editing one another's work, and Chabon reports that he discovered the humor of *Wonder Boys* through Waldman's reaction. His favorite work remains the poem that he wrote for her on their tenth wedding anniversary. In *The Yiddish Policemen's Union*, the detective Meyer Landsman mourns the child that his wife Bina did not carry to full term due to the possibility of a significant birth defect. This poignant part of Landsman's history recalls the heartbreaking decision that Waldman and Chabon made to terminate a high-risk pregnancy. In a chapter of *Bad Mother* titled "Rocketship," the name given to the baby that they chose to abort, Waldman recounts this family tragedy and Chabon's Mother's Day gift to her of a plum sapling that has become known as "Rocketship's Tree."

Chabon's personal life as well as his writing has become progressively more Jewish-centered. Early in his career, he chose the path of assimilation and had no use for his Jewish heritage. However, the failure of *Fountain City*, the death of his grandparents, as well as questions about raising children with his non-Jewish first wife, Lollie Groth, and their subsequent divorce caused him to reevaluate his relationship to Jewishness. This was part of his process to "retrace my steps and see if I dropped anything along the way that might serve me ... better than I had imagined at the time of letting it go" ("Imaginary Homelands," *Maps and Legends*, 190). Writing the reactions of non-Jewish characters to a Passover seder in *Wonder Boys* allowed him indirectly to examine and reconnect with Jewish tradition. As he puts it, "I didn't set out to write a Jewish book, but that's how it worked out" (Brawarsky, 1996). Now it seems to some critics that he "can't seem to stop writing about Jews" (Blume). Chabon finds Judaism's prioritizing of home and family attractive, though he acknowledges that "the thought that you can use Judaism as a way of investing your life with spiritual meaning is an almost bizarrely radical concept" (Judy Oppenheimer). Chabon takes pride in and embraces the label "Jewish writer." Profoundly conscious of the privilege of literary freedom that comes with being a writer in the United States, he nevertheless describes himself as writing "in exile" ("Imaginary Homelands," 169).

As a citizen-artist, Chabon has used his literary celebrity to promote freedom of speech and civic engagement. Notably, Waldman regards her husband as a "natural patriot" (Waldman, *Bad Mother*, 190). Chabon supported George "Julius" T., a student who wrote a poem about school violence that was interpreted as a threat, with an amicus brief. He has served on the advisory board of the First Amendment Project and has organized prominent writers to auction off naming rights for characters as a fundraiser for that group. His essay "Maps and Legends" was reprinted in a post-9/11 anthology, *Writers on America*, distributed abroad by the State Department. Chabon is on the editorial board of the Progressive Book Club, an organization that defines itself as striving to "find the books and showcase the ideas that can change our nation for the better." He participated in Operation Ohio, 2004, a program sponsored by the literary journal *McSweeney's* to remind college students in swing states to vote. He attended the Democratic Convention in 2008 and wrote about that experience for the *New York Review of Books*. Citing Barack Obama as the first presidential candidate he supported with genuine excitement, Chabon admires Obama's writing and identifies with his love for the United States that is accompanied by ambivalence about its history. Chabon's complex historical consciousness as both a Jew and an American is especially well-developed in *The Amazing Adventures of Kavalier and Clay* and *The Yiddish Policemen's Union*. Such consciousness combined with exquisite prose and a love of story has earned Chabon the status of popular literary wonder boy.

DISCUSSION QUESTIONS

- How much does biographical information about an author influence your reading of a novel? What are the differences between fiction and autobiography/memoir?
- How has Chabon's life influenced his choice of subject matter?
- To what extent are Chabon's politics reflected in his fiction?

2

MICHAEL CHABON AND THE NOVEL

Early in his career, Michael Chabon wrote highly praised short stories, yet he found himself frustrated by the lack of diversity of that form and the requisite "epiphanic dew" of his own work (Chabon, "Trickster in a Suit of Lights," *Maps and Legends*, 18). Ultimately, as he explains in "My Back Pages," he "couldn't stop preferring traditional, bourgeois narrative form" (*Maps and Legends*, 148). As a novelist, Chabon is invested in telling stories and creating complex characters. His first three novels—*The Mysteries of Pittsburgh*, *Wonder Boys*, and *The Amazing Adventures of Kavalier and Clay*—share a propensity for coming-of-age narratives that integrate elements of the picaresque and historical fiction. With increasingly explicit Jewish content, Chabon's works are part of the contemporary Jewish literary renaissance. In recent years, Chabon also has embraced genre fiction more explicitly in *The Final Solution*, *The Yiddish Policemen's Union*, and *Gentlemen of the Road*: by using the conventions of detective and adventure stories, Chabon strives to reclaim the value of entertainment for literary fiction and to bring Jewish themes to genres not traditionally associated with such ethnic and religious concerns.

COMING OF AGE THROUGH PICARESQUE ADVENTURES

The coming-of-age-novel is often referred to by its German name, *bildungsroman.* Such narratives chart the development and education of the protagonist. When the maturing youth has artistic inclinations, the novel is termed a *künstlerroman* (German for artist's novel). Some classic coming-of-age novels written in English include Charles Dickens's *David Copperfield*, Charlotte Brontë's *Jane Eyre*, D. H. Lawrence's *Sons and Lovers*, James Joyce's *A Portrait of the Artist as a Young Man*, Mark Twain's *Huckleberry Finn*, J. D. Salinger's *The Catcher in the Rye*, Richard Wright's *Black Boy*, and Toni Morrison's *The Bluest Eye*. In coming-of-age novels, protagonists must form, negotiate, and sometimes repudiate relationships with parents, mentors, peers, and romantic partners. Positioning themselves within their communities, these characters often have to grapple with the gap between their ideals and the conditions of everyday life. Traditionally, protagonists of these novels are talked about as losing their "innocence"; more precisely, however, these characters use the knowledge and experience they have gained to form a revised view of their world and their place and possibilities within it. Sometimes this revised vision is a hopeful one of fulfillment or future potential; sometimes it includes profound cynicism and resignation.

Chabon's first novel, *The Mysteries of Pittsburgh*, chronicles the coming of age of Art Bechstein during the transitional summer after he has completed college. Like many other *bildungsroman* protagonists, Art must negotiate between his own desires and the expectations of his father. While Art's gangster father, Joe the Egg, expects his son to use the economics degree he has just earned to secure a responsible and respectable position, Art's plan is to work as a bookstore clerk and to integrate himself into his new community of stylish and daring friends: Arthur, a poised gay man who welcomes Art into his world; Arthur's hard-drinking boyhood friend, Cleveland, and his girlfriend, Jane; and Phlox, a woman who has undergone many transformations herself. A murky family history in which his mother was murdered years ago by a bullet probably meant for Mr. Bechstein exacerbates Art's struggle with his father. Thus tension and hysteria result whenever his father comes to Pittsburgh for "business" and to see his son. Cleveland's attempt to use his friendship with Art, the "son of a gangster" (*The Mysteries of Pittsburgh*, 62), to advance his own career as a professional criminal furthers the discord between father and son. This summer is also a period of sexual awakening and confusion, as Art becomes romantically involved with both Arthur and Phlox. By the end of the novel, Art has cut himself off from his father after the latter set Cleveland up to be pursued by the police and tried to strong-arm Arthur into leaving Art. This coming-of-age narrative ends with Art's intention to father himself and with his nostalgia for the lost promise of that fateful summer.

Art's summer of development includes some picaresque adventures. The picaresque is a genre that focuses on an antiheroic protagonist known as a picaro; he (or she) refuses to conform to the discipline and stability associated with a virtuous middle-class life and opts instead for a life of wandering and sometimes roguish, delinquent, antisocial behavior. The picaresque protagonist tends to be a social chameleon. In English, the picaresque ranges from Daniel Defoe's eighteenth-century novel *Moll Flanders* and Mark Twain's *Huckleberry Finn* to Jack Kerouac's *On the Road* and Rita Mae Brown's *Rubyfruit Jungle*. Structurally, the picaresque is episodic. Art's wandering from party to party, his accompanying Arthur from one housesitting adventure to another, and his trips on the back of Cleveland's motorcycle through the environs of Pittsburgh exemplify the merger of the *bildungsroman* and the picaresque in *The Mysteries of Pittsburgh*.

According to Arthur, Cleveland was a writer prior to becoming a gangster. Thus, his story might be viewed as a thwarted *künstlerroman* and hints at the transgressive tendencies of would-be writers. In Chabon's second novel, *Wonder Boys*, Grady Tripp and his student, James Leer, function as the dual protagonists of this picaresque *künstlerroman*, a blending of genres that invites reflection on dominant cultural images of writers. At the start of WordFest, the literary festival that takes place during the retrospectively narrated, action-packed weekend of *Wonder Boys*, it becomes clear that both Grady's writing and love lives have devolved. His long overdue fourth novel has developed in length but not in coherence, and he seems capable of delivering only false promises to his editor. His romantic life is an intersecting narrative of chaos: his third marriage is ending, and his mistress, the chancellor of the college where he teaches creative writing, is pregnant. His frequent marijuana-induced highs contribute to the literal and symbolic falls that he experiences throughout the novel.

On the road throughout the weekend, Grady drops off his editor's cross-dressing traveling companion, covers up the shooting of his department chair's dog, recovers a stolen jacket once belonging to Marilyn Monroe, rescues James from his family home, and attends the Passover seder hosted by the parents of his Korean American Jewish wife. Ultimately, chance, which takes the form of the winds of Pittsburgh, liberates Grady from his failed novel. The retrospective narration of *Wonder Boys* ends with Grady's report that he has quit his cannibis habit for a settled life as a father and husband with a regular writing routine. The devolved picaro–writer has developed into a responsible family man and teacher.

While Grady Tripp is a portrait of the writer as a middle-aged man, James Leer, as a youthful up-and-coming writer, is a more conventional protagonist for a *künstlerroman*. Self-fashioning himself in the image of a dark, brooding solitary writer, James is obsessed with Hollywood suicides, and his creative writing classmates view his work with scorn. Signaling not only his talent but also his antisocial tendencies, he spins yarns about his own impoverished status. James is discovered to have a promising manuscript titled *The Love Parade*. By the end of the novel, James is romantically involved with Terry Crabtree, Grady's male editor, who is set to publish James's book. Thus James's narrative of development as a writer becomes aligned with his sexual awakening and his coming-out story. In a cross-generational narrative of the rise and fall of writerly wonder boys, James and Grady mentor one another as they travel from one adventure to another in a car whose trunk is weighed down with a tuba, a crushed boa constrictor, and a dead dog. The picaresque elements of this novel provide an ironically comic edge to this *künstlerroman*, while the Passover seder at the heart of the novel becomes Chabon's means of writing his way into the Jewish American novel.

HISTORY AND ARTISTIC DEVELOPMENT

As the title suggests, *The Amazing Adventures of Kavalier and Clay* also features dual protagonists: Sammy Clay of Brooklyn and his cousin, Josef (Joe) Kavalier, émigré from Nazi-occupied Prague. Historical forces shape the development of these two young men as comic book artists— Sammy as writer, Joe as illustrator. Escaping from the European catastrophe known as the Holocaust, Joe is an art student who arrives in New York desperate to make money to secure the freedom of his family in Prague; Sammy is looking for a partner who will help him to fill the void left by his father's abandonment; and the United States is desperate for superheroes who might provide a worldview conducive to winning a world war against dictatorship and genocide.

The low-prestige, developing comic book industry is one of the few creative commercial outlets open to Jews. However, even in comic books, the Golem, a figure from Jewish legend and Joe's first image of a superhero, is pronounced "too Jewish." Thus, through conversation, Kavalier and Clay's Escapist is born. Representing the League of the Golden Key, this superhero seeks to defeat the oppressive forces of the Iron Chain. For a time, Joe fights the war vicariously through his comic book creation; one controversial cover depicts the Escapist delivering a blow to Hitler's jaw. Joe ultimately must accept both the healing escapism of art as well as the limits of art's power to save those bodies and cultures perishing at the hands of historical and militarily powerful villains. By the end of the novel, he produces a graphic novel about the Golem that memorializes his now forever lost Prague home and family. Thus, Joe's artistic development becomes an explicitly Jewish narrative. While in *My Name is Asher Lev* Chaim Potok creates a *künstlerroman* about a traditionally observant Jewish artist, Chabon's Jewish portrait of an artist is a decidedly secular tale, and Joe experiences no contradiction between his commitments to Jewish themes and his daily ingestion of an unkosher pork chop.

In sharp contrast to Joe, who has an abiding faith in the legitimacy of comic books as an art form, Sammy feels torn between the popular comic book creations and genre fiction that earn him a living and the "serious" novel, *American Disillusionment,* that he works on sporadically throughout his career. This attitude is consistent with the worldview of his only mentor, Mr. Deasey, an embittered, cynical genre fiction writer convinced of the unbridgeable chasm between high and low art forms and thus filled with disdain for his own literary output. As the Senate Subcommittee to Investigate Juvenile Delinquency points out in its hearings on comic books, Sammy tends to create superheroes that have young male sidekicks. While that governmental body considers such conventions an indirect homoerotic narrative and a coded avowal of Sammy's gay desires, Sammy considers such tendencies to be a son's longing for a father. Thus, Sammy's development and trials as an artist give voice to the strict compartmentalizing of not only the popular and the aesthetic but also the homosexual and the heterosexual.

The artistic development of Rosa Saks, Joe's great love who becomes Sammy's wife, suggests the difference that gender can make in the *künstlerroman.* Initially, Rose is the object of Joe's artistic gaze, and her surrealistic sketches in combination with his desire for her become fodder for his creation of voluptuous female superheroes, notably Luna Moth. In the last large-scale painting that Rosa produces, she depicts Joe in chains and herself as holding the Golden Key; hence her artistic and romantic powers are codependent. Later, as Sammy's wife, she becomes a substitute for Joe and partners with Sammy on some of his comic book series. Her creations become an outlet for her romantic longings and an escape from the boredom that she experiences as a postwar suburban housewife.

The last section of this epic novel includes the beginnings of the coming-of-age narrative of Tommy, Rosa's son who is the biological offspring of Joe adopted by Sammy. Notably, Tommy is the one who connects with Joe and returns him to Rosa and Sammy. Rather than repudiating the father as Art does in *The Mysteries of Pittsburgh,* Tommy brings him home. Tommy also seems to follow in both his fathers' creative footsteps by imagining for himself a comic book alter ego, the Bug. Ultimately, *The Amazing Adventures of Kavalier and Clay* weds the *künstlerroman* to the historical novel. Here, individual, familial, and aesthetic development become interwoven with the history of comic books and attendant aesthetic debates, with divergent national histories of anti-Semitism, and with histories of gender and sexuality before the second wave of feminism and before the contemporary gay rights movement that began with the Stonewall riots in New York City in 1969.

JEWISH GENRE FICTION

Michael Chabon's decision to "come out" as a literary practitioner of genre fiction in *The Final Solution, The Yiddish Policemen's Union,* and *Gentlemen of the Road* is consonant with Joe Kavalier's belief that popular genres and aesthetic value can and do coexist. Genre fiction refers to such popular, sometimes overlapping forms as romance, adventure, mystery, science fiction, and the hard-boiled detective story. In *The Final Solution,* Chabon maps a Holocaust narrative onto the form of the mystery. In this work, the detective is none other than a quite aged, though unnamed, Sherlock Holmes. The famed detective created by Sir Arthur Conan Doyle is indebted to Edgar Allan Poe's detective Dupin, who appears in such famous stories as "The Murders in the Rue Morgue" and "The Purloined Letter"; successors to Conan Doyle's Holmes include Agatha Christie's Detective Poirot and Miss Marple. For Holmes's fans, the detective in *The Final Solution* is recognizable from Chabon's allusions to his reputation as well as to his beekeeping activities. A further authorial clue to the detective's identity is the very title *The Final Solution,* which refers to Conan Doyle's "The Final Problem" as well as to Nicholas Meyer's novel about Holmes titled *The Seven-Per-Cent Solution.* Of course, the title *The Final Solution* also refers to the Nazis' plan to eradicate the Jewish people; hence, at the outset, it becomes clear that this mystery also contributes to the strand of the Jewish American novel that concerns itself with the Holocaust and more specifically with Jewish refugee/survivor figures. This tradition includes Edward Wallant's *The Pawnbroker,* Cynthia Ozick's *The Shawl,* and Saul Bellow's *Mr. Sammler's Planet* as well as more recent texts such as Thane Rosenbaum's *Second Hand Smoke,* Aryeh Lev Stollman's *The Far Euphrates,* and Chabon's own *The Amazing Adventures of Kavalier and Clay.*

In Chabon's *The Final Solution,* Linus Steinman is a young boy who has escaped from Nazi-occupied Europe to the English countryside and

has been traumatized into silence. His pet parrot and constant companion, Bruno, is at the heart of the mystery and violence of the novella.
Bruno regularly recites in German a series of numbers, the meaning and
value of which is an enigma to those assembled in the Panicker boarding house. When Mr. Shane, a new arrival at the Panickers', is found
dead (a dead body being a requirement for this genre) and Linus's
Bruno is abducted, Mr. Holmes is ousted from retirement. Upstaging
the police investigation, as is his wont, he proves that the suspect in
custody, the delinquent son of the boarding house owners, is not the
culprit. He then uses his powers of deduction to find the real killer
and to restore the parrot to Linus. However, his success here is uncon-
ventionally limited, as he avers the impossibility of ever deciphering
Bruno's numerical code. Yet Linus and the parrot, who narrates a section of this work, know that Bruno's numbers are a train song sung in
the voice of Linus's mother. By adopting and adapting the conventions
of the Sherlock Holmes mystery, Chabon demonstrates the powerlessness of Enlightenment reason to comprehend fully the horrors and
losses of the Holocaust.

In *The Yiddish Policemen's Union*, Chabon uses the conventions of
the hard-boiled detective story to chronicle an alternative afterlife of
the Holocaust. The action-packed plot of hard-boiled detective fiction
revolves around investigating the mysterious circumstances that attend a
violent death. Place has the force of character in this genre, and the
conventional terrain is the dark, "mean streets" of urban areas. A lone,
often vulnerable detective is charged with solving the crime, but the
darkness of the moral landscape of the hard-boiled world is unlikely to
be appreciably lightened by the resolution of the case. According to
Raymond Chandler, one of the great hard-boiled writers, the detective
figure in such fiction is necessarily "a common man." Chandler's formulation reflects the male bent of the genre; although more female hard-
boiled detectives have appeared recently, the femme fatale has been the
conventional female type associated with this form. Short sentences and
spare language are the stylistic markers of the genre and are meant to
reflect the muscular values of the depicted world. Dashiell Hammett's
The Maltese Falcon and Chandler's *The Long Goodbye* are classics of
the genre; Chabon reports rereading the latter while at work on *The
Yiddish Policemen's Union*.

The Yiddish policeman of the title is Meyer Landsman; his last name,
which in Yiddish means an Eastern European countryman, underscores
his status as a "Jewish everyman" (Schifrin). The place of the novel is
Sitka, Alaska, where Jews fleeing the Holocaust took refuge and made a
temporary home after the Jewish state of Israel was decimated in 1948;

sixty years later, Sitka is "reverting" to U.S. control, and it becomes time for most of Sitka's Jews to wander once again.

Playfully paying homage to the genre, Chabon depicts the hard-drinking Meyer as afraid of the dark. The suspicious death of the chess-playing, heroin-addicted Mendel Shpilman, son of the Verbov rabbi and a prodigy with messianic potential, takes Meyer into an ultra-Orthodox crime world determined to reestablish the Temple in Jerusalem with the help of evangelical U.S. government agents. Meyer spends a great deal of time alone uncovering the relationship between Mendel's death and that of his pilot-sister Naomi; at crucial moments, however, Meyer is aided by his partner, Berko Shemets, an observant Jew who is half-Tinglit, and by Meyer's ex-wife, Bina Gelbfish.

Meyer's frequent injuries underscore his physical vulnerability, and emotionally he mourns not only the loss of Bina but also their unborn son, aborted because he was at risk for a serious birth defect. In keeping with genre conventions, Chabon's sentences and chapters are much shorter here than in previous works. The genre's emphasis on place enables Chabon to create Sitka as an imagined Yiddishland; thus, he meditates upon and re-creates the Yiddish-centered worlds lost in the Holocaust and muses on the development of Jewish peoplehood had the Hebrew-centered Jewish state of Israel not come into being in the post–World War II era. In Chabon's fictional world, an established Jewish homeland remains only a future possibility, and Sitka "Yids" are necessarily diasporic—dispersed and/or exiled—Jews. Here the hard-boiled detective story becomes uncharacteristically enmeshed with fundamental questions of Jewish history and identity.

Chabon's working title for *Gentlemen of the Road* was "Jews with Swords." His recognition that such a formulation seems not only humorous but also oxymoronic indicates that the overlapping adventure/picaresque genres to which *Gentlemen* is indebted are not conventionally Jewish forms. Escape and travel, especially to rediscover lost worlds, are endemic to the adventure story; in league with the picaresque, adventure happens on the road, and adventurers are outlaw figures. In his Jewish adventure story, Chabon has two gentlemen buddies, Amram and Zelikman, on the move. The violence of a pogrom and antagonism between father and son wrest Zelikman from his Frankish home (in what today would be Germany). The kidnapping of a daughter and the fruitless search for her motivate Amram to roam the world with Mother-Defiler, his sword.

True to genre form, *Gentlemen of the Road* is episodic. In part to reap monetary rewards and in part to visit the fabled Jewish Khazar kingdom, the endearing horse thieves and swindler protagonists of this tale strive to return a member of the ousted ruling family to Khazaria. Along the way, they meet Rhadanite traders, form coalitions with Muslim regiments against marauding Northmen, lose and find treasured hats and horses, in particular a stallion named Hillel who seems to have the wisdom of his rabbinical namesake. Notably, Zelikman chooses life whenever he can, in keeping with the healing arts that he learned from his father and grandfather. Thus, when he comes upon the fallen Hanukkah, he puts his lancet to surgical use, and when he needs to overcome a guard, he does so not with deadly force but rather with chloroform. As in *The Yiddish Policemen's Union*, *Gentlemen of the Road* uses genre fiction as a vehicle for exploring alternative Jewish worlds. Chabon allies the chosen travels of the picaro-adventurer with the often enforced wanderings of diasporic Jews, while simultaneously imagining Jewish self-determination in the half-mythic, multicultural world of the Khazars.

Chabon has used both genre fiction and the coming-of-age novel to express and expand his commitments to the Jewish American tradition. Calling upon conventions of the *künstlerroman*, the picaresque, and the detective story, Chabon's career is a case study of the ways in which genres not only can overlap but also undergo transformation.

DISCUSSION QUESTIONS

- Popular genres are often assumed to be inferior literature. To what extent and in what ways does Chabon's work refute this assumption?
- Are novels that trace the development of an artist of interest to those of us who are not writers or painters? Why and how?
- Do Chabon's later, explicitly Jewish-centered novels strike you as a new direction for him or a continuation of trends in his earlier fiction?

3

THE MYSTERIES OF PITTSBURGH
(1988)

The Mysteries of Pittsburgh, Chabon's first novel originally written as his master's thesis, chronicles Art Bechstein coming of age during the summer after college. This sexually explicit text details a young man's confused desires for love, friendship, and family history. Page numbers cited from *The Mysteries of Pittsburgh* are from the 2000 paperback edition (New York: Perennial).

NARRATIVE SUMMARY

Retrospectively and episodically narrated in the first person by Art Bechstein, the novel opens with strained lunch conversation between Art and his Jewish gangster father. Art's vague and unambitious plans for the summer contribute to the tension of this meeting. Finishing up an essay on Sigmund Freud's correspondence with Wilhelm Fliess, Art gets his first glimpse of Phlox Lombardi and Arthur Lecomte, both of whom work in the library. When Art leaves the library, he witnesses a fight on the street resulting from a love triangle. Arthur, too, is a bystander; he and Art exchange sardonic comments about this scene, go off together to have a beer, and then end up at a party. There Art learns about the legendary Cleveland Arning and meets Jane Bellwether, Cleveland's girlfriend. When Arthur invites Art to a gay dance club, the latter identifies himself as straight despite his history of "sexual doubt" (40) and his attraction to Arthur.

Art moves to another apartment and finds himself newly aroused by the sights and possibilities of Pittsburgh, which include Arthur as well as Phlox, to whom Arthur introduces Art. Lunching with Arthur on a precipice overlooking such iconic landmarks as the Cloud Factory and the Lost Neighborhood, Art identifies strongly with Arthur, hears stories about Cleveland, an alcoholic bad boy, and vows never to become as small as those Pittsburgh citizens he looks down upon from these heights with Arthur.

Working at a low-brow bookstore, Art finds himself haunted by specters of homosexuality. Cleveland arrives on his bike to take Art to the Bellwether home, where Arthur is house-sitting. In keeping with his reputation, Cleveland orchestrates a mating between a trio of pit bulls and Happy, the Bellwethers' neurotic dog. The Bellwethers arrive home unexpectedly. In a farcical attempt to keep Cleveland permanently away from Jane, Mrs. Bellwether tells Cleveland that his girlfriend has died. Expelled from the Bellwethers', Arthur goes home with Art, kisses him, and then apologizes. The next day, a well-dressed Arthur and Phlox meet Art after work and the three go to a bar; Art and Phlox leave together, establishing themselves as a couple. At dinner with his father the next night, Art tells him about Phlox; his father's disapproval reduces him to tears.

Art's relationship with Phlox develops. At one point, he becomes uncomfortable with, though also aroused by, the erotic play that accompanies her reading aloud her favorite book, *The Story of O*. Art's relationship with Cleveland also develops. At the Arning home one night, Art narrates the history of this troubled family, including the suicide of Cleveland's mother, the father's affairs with men, and Cleveland's almost blinding his younger sister in a fit of generalized rage. Art, Arthur, and Cleveland spend a weekend at the Arnings' summer house, where Art sees a picture of a younger and happier Cleveland, and Arthur details Cleveland's deterioration. Cleveland and Art share their respective fantasies of the "will-to-bigness" (129), and Cleveland expresses his desire to meet Art's gangster father so that he might find a more lucrative position in the criminal world. Jane arrives at the summer house, she and Cleveland fight, and Jane, anxious about Cleveland, tries to get information about his activities from Art.

When Art returns to Pittsburgh, he and Phlox play Twister, and he falls. Tension grows between Phlox and Arthur. Art and Arthur spend a day at a country club where Art, years before, had spent time with his now dead mother. When they return to Art's apartment, a phone call from Art's father interrupts a potentially intimate moment between the two young men.

Art brings Phlox to the next dinner meeting he has with his father; she asks Mr. Bechstein all about Art's mother, and Art's father is appalled that Art has not shared memories of his mother with her. "Uncle" Stern, one of his father's criminal associates, and "Aunt" Elaine unexpectedly join this dinner party already under way; they reminisce about Marjorie, Art's mother. Art becomes physically ill and leaves the dinner table.

Cleveland collects debts for Frankie Breezy and takes Art on his collection rounds; with the help of two other thugs, he stages an assault on an old man. Simply by uttering the word "stop," Art interrupts this attack and demonstrates his power as the son of Joe the Egg, aka Mr. Bechstein. Cleveland insists that Art introduce him to his father; they interrupt a "business" meeting under way in Mr. Bechstein's hotel room, which includes Frankie Breezy, Cleveland's current boss, and Carl "Poon" Punicki, a competitor of Breezy's in the fencing of jewels. Mr. Bechstein is enraged that Art has become mixed up with the likes of Cleveland. Upset that the barrier between the world of his friends and the world of his family has been eroded, Art seeks comfort from Arthur and they have intercourse. Phlox learns that Arthur and Art are lovers; she responds with a letter in which she espouses the unnaturalness of intimate relations between men. Cleveland stops by Art's apartment and advises him that he can't love both Arthur and Phlox. Cleveland also informs Art that he is learning to disengage alarm systems so that he can steal jewels. Punicki, his new boss, will then fence these stolen goods.

Art continues his affair with Arthur and avoids his father; he also meets Arthur's mother, a cleaning woman. Thus, Art discovers that all of his assumptions about Arthur's privileged background are wrong and that his lover has invented himself.

Meanwhile, Phlox engineers a meeting with Art in the library; they become lovers again and have anal intercourse. Art's sexual confusion mounts, and he meets Arthur to tell him about his latest encounter with Phlox. Distraught, Arthur begs Art not to leave him; bereft of his usual aplomb, Arthur confesses that he has failed the Foreign Service exam and that his life is in disarray.

With the title *The Mysteries of Pittsburgh*, Chabon riffs on *The Mysteries of Paris*, a nineteenth-century French novel by Eugene Sue that features a duke disguised as a worker. Short chapters with pithy titles such as "Thou Shalt Not Lust" and "An Unexpected Friend" mark this serialized novel.

In the penultimate chapter, Cleveland engages in a jewel heist for his new boss; however, the police had been alerted, by order of Joe the Egg Bechstein, to the planned crime. On the run from the police, Cleveland enlists Art's help. When a helicopter appears, Cleveland climbs to the summit of the Cloud Factory, clutching the doll in which he has hidden the stolen jewels. From this height, he creates an enormous shadow and then falls to his death. Distraught, Art seeks to evade the grasp of the officer who guards him; he wakes up in a hospital room, suffering from the effects of the head blows he received from that officer. "Uncle" Lenny is at the hospital, and Art asks him about the death of his mother. When Joe arrives, Art refuses to see him. He checks out of the hospital, returns to his apartment, and finds Arthur there. Art's male lover has been told to leave town by Joe Bechstein's people (Art had been outed by Phlox's letter, which Cleveland had in his possession when he died). In the final pages, Art details his travels and breakup with Arthur as well as the account he received of Cleveland's funeral.

CHARACTERS

Art Bechstein is the narrator of *The Mysteries of Pittsburgh*. He retrospectively recounts the summer after college in which he experiences intimate relationships with both a man and a woman, and becomes immersed in the gangster world of his father from which he has previously been shielded. Although he seeks to join the seemingly superior world of beautiful people, he must resign himself to the loss of friendship, love, and family by the end of the novel.

Joe Bechstein, aka Joe the Egg, is Art's impeccably polite gangster father who manages the finances of the Maggio crime family. After the murder of his wife, he becomes protective of Art and strives to ensure that his son has a very different life from his own. His relationship with his son is a tense and formal one consisting of ritual dinners and movie outings; his disapproval has the effect of reducing Art to tears. He tries to control/protect Art by setting up Cleveland and threatening Arthur, but these actions cause Art to cut off relations with Joe and to father himself.

As a young boy, Art was obsessed with his father's "secret identity," and his youthful imagination caused him to search repeatedly for his father's "multicolored superhero (or supervillain) costume" (*Mysteries*, 19). Here Chabon provides a glimpse of the comic book imagination given full play in *The Amazing Adventures of Kavalier and Clay*.

Lenny Stern is one of Joe's close gangster associates and is known as "Uncle" Lenny. He represents a source of family knowledge and history. He appears when Art and Phlox are having dinner with Joe and further blurs the boundary between the world of Art's friends and the world of his family. When Art is in the hospital, Lenny strives to reassure him; however, such assertions of protection and comfort ring especially hollow to Art after Cleveland's death.

Elaine Stern is Lenny's wife and is known as "Aunt" Elaine. Her affection for Art is portrayed as excessive and painful; growing up, he nicknamed her "the Pincher" (177).

Phlox Lombardi is Art's female lover. The library office in which she works is behind a window grille. Thus, she is "the Girl Behind Bars" (13), a sign that she is an imprisoned and imprisoning figure. She is chameleon-like; both the punk and Christian scene have been part of her repertoire, and she is unduly influenced by movie stars and the literature that she consumes as a French major. Alternately and sometimes simultaneously alluring and terrifying to Art, she is in competition with Arthur for Art's affection; she is also intensely homophobic.

Riri, a young Iranian woman, hosts the party to which Arthur takes Art. Exoticized by Art, Riri and the scene at her home represent the exciting, erotic, cosmopolitan world that he strives to join. However, the transformations of objects, including the swimming pool, which occur during the course of Riri's party suggest that this world is less glamorous and more complicated than it initially appears.

Mohammad, aka Momo, is a friend and sometime lover of Arthur. Driving a green Audi, he takes Arthur and Art to Riri's party. Originally from Lebanon, he, like Riri, is portrayed as part of an exotic, global, jet-setting crowd. At the party, a love triangle constituted by Momo, Arthur, and a man named Richard is the cause of some tension.

Arthur Lecomte is a gay man who becomes Art's lover. A would-be diplomat, he styles himself as a "free agent—a free atom" (28); affected, affable, but ultimately aloof, he introduces Art to Phlox and constitutes the third member of that love triangle. Art both wants to be like and with Arthur. However, when Art meets Arthur's mother, he realizes that, as a worldly elitist, Arthur is "largely his own invention" (248).

Marjorie Bechstein was Art's mother. She was murdered, probably by a bullet intended for Joe. She is one of the many subjects about which Art and his father don't talk. An absence that haunts Art and the novel, "Marjorie" is the title of a chapter.

Cleveland Arning has the class origins to which Arthur aspires but styles himself as a biker rebel/gangster. He was a writer but has turned into a charming, manipulative, and self-destructive alcoholic. His relationship with Jane, whom he seems to truly love, is tumultuous. He is ultimately a tragic figure.

Jane Bellwether is Cleveland's girlfriend. Beautiful and poised, she initially attracts Art's interest as a potential portal to and prize in Arthur's world. The passionate intimacy between Cleveland and Jane evokes feelings of envy and belatedness in Art. Jane loves Cleveland but also fears for him. Although therapy sessions filled with family woe are mentioned, she is an opaque character.

Mrs. Lecomte is Arthur's mother. She is a cleaning woman and thus contradicts Arthur's carefully cultivated image. Like Art's father, she is a figure to be kept separate from her son's world and friends; indeed, when she comes to one of the homes at which he house-sits, he tries to get rid of her as quickly as possible, even as Art tries to learn more about Arthur's "terrific secret" (21). Arthur strives to torment his staunchly Catholic mother with ritualized blasphemy, despite his own inclination to attend Mass.

Happy, the ironically named Bellwether dog, bears the emotional scars of being abused by the neurotic Nettie Bellwether. When Happy is in heat, Cleveland orchestrates her mating with three pit bulls owned by a neighbor boy. For the Bellwethers, the defiling of Happy is analogous to Cleveland's relationship with their daughter Jane as well as a clear sign of his degeneracy.

Nettie Bellwether, Jane's mother, is portrayed as the bane of the Bellwether household. Under her care and tutelage and as a result of literal hammering, even the family dog becomes a physical and emotional wreck. Not a subtle character, she baldly lies about her own daughter's death.

Dr. Cleveland Arning is Cleveland's father, a psychiatrist who lived a secret life with other men. He installed an elevator in their home, making the action of rising and falling a literal as well as symbolic part of the Arning household. Notably, Art's fantasy of "bigness" involves an elevator. Art and Cleveland become linked through Dr. Arning, just as they become linked through Joe and his gangster world.

Mrs. Arning is Cleveland's mother. The wife of a man who loved other men, she committed suicide. Like Art, Cleveland is haunted by his absent mother.

Anna Arning is Cleveland's younger sister, one of his first fans and victims. In a fit of displaced rage, he almost drowns her and then nearly blinds her. She represents the dangers of loving Cleveland. Art comes upon her empty bedroom when he stays the night at the Arning household. Anna is another absent female figure who haunts the novel.

Frankie Breezy is a gangster who employs Cleveland to collect debts and the astronomical interest that accrues on money owed to mobsters. He, too, is in Joe's hotel room when Cleveland, looking for a more lucrative job, meets both Art's father and Poon. Breezy is also Poon's competitor. Thus, he has ample reason to delight in Joe's order that Cleveland be disciplined for stepping out of line and, more importantly, for involving Art in the criminal world from which Joe has shielded his son. Breezy sets Cleveland up to be apprehended by the police and hence is a catalyst for his death.

Carl "Poon" Punicki is a member of the gangster underworld whom Cleveland meets in Joe's hotel room. Poon hires Cleveland to steal jewels that he can fence. Poon and Frankie Breezy compete for the same black market territory. The chapter titled "The Big P" ostensibly refers to Edgar Allan Poe, whose writings Cleveland carries in his pocket; however, Poon is another "Big P." For Cleveland, the art of stealing jewels competes with and dominates the art of narrative.

Pete Arcola is Cleveland's mentor in the art of jewel theft. He deems Cleveland as having great potential. Notably, Pete was a member of the U.S. Army's Special Forces. Arcola, like Art's father, establishes continuity between the criminal world and respected masculine institutions.

THEMES

In *The Mysteries of Pittsburgh*, the mysteries and secrets of identity are dominant thematic elements developed through Joe's secret life as a gangster and Arthur's as the son of a cleaning woman. The extent to which we can fashion ourselves apart from family history becomes a crucial question. Of course, the mysteries and secrets of identity are also fundamentally sexual; thus, Art, exploring the porous boundaries that shape heterosexual, homosexual, and bisexual desires, ricochets between Phlox and Arthur. Loss—of parents, of friends, of lovers, of possibilities for one's self—also feature prominently in the novel. Relatedly, *The Mysteries of Pittsburgh* revels in and indicts nostalgia as a lifestyle, in part through the cinematic allusions sprinkled throughout the text.

Chabon's debut novel explores the diversity, intensity, and complexity of relations between men. Both Art and Cleveland have fraught histories with their fathers, and the novel poignantly portrays the betrayals and disappointments that fathers and sons visit upon one another. Male friendships, such as that between Art and Cleveland, are similarly vexed. The homophobia displayed by both Phlox and Joe Bechstein points to the cultural prohibitions that can keep men from expressing their love for one another, sexually or otherwise. The loyalty and violence that mark the world of gangsters in *The Mysteries of Pittsburgh* are continuous with the mixture of pleasure and pain that characterizes male-male relationships in this novel and those that follow.

DISCUSSION QUESTIONS

- Do you regard Art as a reliable narrator? Why or why not?
- Which chapter titles seem to summarize not only their respective chapter but also the novel as a whole?
- Which of these characters would you like to count among your friends? Which would you consider potentially toxic?
- What are the effects of having one character called Art and another Arthur?

4

WONDER BOYS
(1995)

Michael Chabon's second novel, *Wonder Boys*, chronicles the travails of Grady Tripp, a pot-smoking writer whose out-of-control appetite for words, images, and sprawling histories of characters and places renders him unable to finish *Wonder Boys*, the novel that he has been reworking for years. The title overlap between Chabon's published novel and Grady's unfinished work suggests both the affinity and sharp distinction between author and character. Page numbers cited from *Wonder Boys* are from the 2008 paperback edition (New York: Random House Trade Paperbacks).

NARRATIVE SUMMARY

The novel begins with Grady Tripp's first-person retrospective narration about one of his models for a writer, August Van Zorn, aka Albert Vetch. Van Zorn was a Gothic genre writer whose family died tragically. Suffering from the "midnight disease," the insomnia-like alienation that plagues writers, Van Zorn eventually killed himself in the hotel room he rented from Grady's grandmother. Grady was raised by his grandmother because his own mother died in his infancy. Grady's father, a policeman, committed suicide after mistaking one of the few Jews in the town for a robbery suspect and killing him.

Grady ultimately focuses on the weekend of a particularly memorable WordFest, a literary festival held annually at the Pittsburgh college where he teaches creative writing. The Friday of that festival, Grady is dealing with the chaos of his life and writing: his third wife, Emily, has left him; and his editor, Terry Crabtree, is arriving in Pittsburgh to read Grady's long-overdue novel. Despite Grady's claims to the contrary and the 2,000-plus pages of manuscript he has written under the habitual influence of marijuana, his novel *Wonder Boys* is nowhere near complete.

When Crabtree arrives at the airport, he is accompanied by Antonia Sloviak, whom Grady recognizes as a transgender woman; included among the luggage deposited in Grady's trunk is a tuba. This becomes part of the baggage that travels with Grady throughout the novel. Crabtree, whom Grady has known since college when they both discovered their shared knowledge of August Van Zorn's fiction, reveals that his editorial job is in jeopardy. The first party of the festival is held at the home of the Gaskells. Sara Gaskell is the chancellor of Grady's college and his lover; Walter Gaskell, Sara's husband, chairs the English department, Grady's academic unit.

Early in the evening, Sara manages a private moment with Grady and informs him that she is pregnant. Overwhelmed by the events of the day and the cannibis he has consumed, he wanders outside and discovers one of his students, James Leer, lurking in the dark. Earlier in the day, Grady's creative writing workshop had savagely critiqued James's writing. At the end of the session, preoccupied by his own troubles, Grady left James alone in a dark classroom. Now, seeing a depressed James with a small pistol in his possession, Grady convinces him to join the party, to which he had not been invited.

At the party, Crabtree is attracted to James and makes advances toward him. Grady brings James upstairs to the Gaskells' bedroom and unlocks the safe to Walter Gaskell's memorabilia collection, which includes the jacket that Marilyn Monroe wore when she married Joe DiMaggio. James, an old movie buff and an expert on Hollywood suicides, is moved by the sight of the jacket. Grady leaves the bedroom before James and is attacked by Doctor Dee, the Gaskell family dog. James shoots and kills the dog. Grady and James carry Doctor Dee to Grady's car; the canine corpse now joins the tuba in the trunk. In Crabtree's garment bag, Grady locates the drugs and alcohol that his old friend usually has on hand, and both Grady and James partake.

At WordFest, the writer "Q" gives a lecture on the double life of a writer who commits outlandish and often self-destructive acts in order to provide material for a literary life. James becomes ill; Sara, in her role as administrator, tends to him. Crabtree and Hannah Green, an attractive student of Grady's who lives in his basement apartment, take charge of James. Grady drives a jilted and distraught Antonia to the home of her parents; on the way, in the green Galaxie that Grady has recently acquired, Antonia transforms herself into Tony, the son that her parents are expecting.

Grady meets up with Hannah, Crabtree and James at the Hi-Hat, an edgy bar that has history for Grady and Crabtree. There the old college friends notice a man with a pompadour and a scar; they name him Vernon Hardapple and begin to narrate a story about him. Although James was assumed to be unconscious, he contributes to this narrative. Later that evening, Hannah drives James to Grady's home to sleep off the effects of the evening. As Grady and Crabtree leave the Hi-Hat, the man dubbed Vernon Hardapple appears. Claiming that Grady's car belongs to him, he jumps on the hood, leaving a dent in the shape of his buttocks. When Grady retrieves the knapsack that James left behind in the auditorium where "Q" gave his lecture, he discovers that it contains not only *The Love Parade*, a novel that James has written, but also the valuable Marilyn Monroe jacket that belongs to Walter Gaskell.

The next morning Grady must deal with a policeman investigating a robbery at the Gaskells' house as well as their missing dog. Grady feigns ignorance of these events. He and a severely hungover James venture out to the Gaskells' to provide explanations and to return the jacket. However, Grady, indecisive about Sara's pregnancy and their future as a couple, shifts plans. With James in tow, he leaves for Kinship, where the Warshaws, his wife's family, will host a Passover seder that evening. On the road, James provides an origin story of growing up impoverished and alienated in a small town. When they arrive in Kinship, Irv Warshaw, Emily's father, tends to Grady's infected, dog-bitten ankle. While James plays a game of beer pong with Phil, Emily's brother, Grady tells Deborah, Emily's sister, about Sara's pregnancy. At the seder, Emily sits next to Grady. The Warshaws are a multicultural Jewish family. Irv and Irene Warshaw have adopted Korean orphans and raised them as Jews; Sam, their only son by birth, drowned, and the anniversary of his death is marked by a memorial candle that burns in a small glass. Phil's wife, Marie, has converted to Judaism and has a great deal of religious knowledge that the more culturally oriented Warshaws lack.

At the Passover seder, the Warshaws discuss a documentary about Jews who aspire to rebuild the Temple in Jerusalem. This detail points back to the plot of *Fountain City*, the novel Chabon never completed, and anticipates a major narrative thread of *The Yiddish Policemen's Union*.

Although farce continually threatens this seder, James Leer, the youngest person at the table, reads with feeling the four questions that establish the distinctive features of the ritual meal accompanying the retelling of the Exodus story; all are moved by his recitation. However, chaos soon erupts. James, who had already drunk a great deal during the beer pong game with Phil, dutifully drinks the four glasses of wine that are part of the ritual meal and passes out. Mrs. Warshaw puts him to bed and calls his parents to pick him up. Deborah instigates an argument with Emily and then tells her about Sara's pregnancy; Emily, who had tried to get pregnant years before with Grady, drives off before the seder ends. When the Leers finally arrive, it becomes obvious that this couple, probably his grandparents, are quite wealthy and that the life narrative James delivered to Grady is a compelling piece of fiction. After James unwillingly leaves with Fred and Amanda Leer, Grady finds that his student once again has left behind the knapsack that contains Monroe's jacket and his manuscript. Grady reads James's *The Love Parade* and feels jealous "mostly of his simply having *finished* his book" (250). Leaving the Warshaws at Emily's behest, Grady runs over the family's boa constrictor. The dead snake joins the dead dog and the tuba in Grady's trunk.

When Grady returns home, he finds a party going on without him and Crabtree angry at having been left alone all day and now adrift at an evening gathering in which everyone is straight. Uneasy about abandoning James to his guardians, Grady enlists Crabtree as his partner in liberating James from their clutches. The two drive to the magisterial Leer house in the posh suburbs of Pittsburgh where James resides in the basement that he has adorned with a shrine to Frank Capra, the movie director, and suicidal Hollywood idols, including Marilyn Monroe. While James and Crabtree wait in the car, Grady takes the dead dog out of his trunk and puts it under James's blanket as a decoy. Grady discovers that James has begun a short story about the seder and has stolen Sam's yartzheit (memorial) candle. On the way back to Grady's house, James reports that his family shed their Jewish origins and that he didn't feel Jewish at the seder but rather felt that he was nothing.

The next morning Grady talks to Hannah about *Wonder Boys*, since she read part of it the night before. Although she strives to be charitable, she can't help but point out the disjointed nature of the work and the fact that narrative descriptions sans characters sometimes ensue for forty pages. She also suggests that his novel might be more coherent if he weren't always stoned while writing. When a policeman comes looking for James, Grady discovers that he and Crabtree have spent a passionate night together; the usually ironic Crabtree obviously feels tenderness for the young man and wants to help him. Grady allows the officer to take James to meet with the Gaskells and promises to follow shortly with the stolen jacket. However, the jacket is in the Galaxie, which has been repossessed by its rightful owner, Peterson Walker, otherwise known as Vernon Hardapple. Borrowing Hannah's car, Grady and Crabtree track the Galaxie down by first going back to the Hi-Hat bar and then to the sporting goods store where Walker works. A fight ensues. While Crabtree tries to steer Hannah's car out of an alley with the door open, most of the pages of Grady's manuscript scatter to the winds.

The two drive back to the college to find James and the Gaskells. On the way, Grady mourns the loss of his manuscript—only seven pages remain—and realizes that Crabtree has no intention of publishing *Wonder Boys*, although he does plan to save his own career and to launch James's by publishing *The Love Parade*. When they reach the college, Crabtree takes control. At the final event of WordFest, to which Grady arrives late, Crabtree's plan to publish not only James's novel but also Walter Gaskell's critical study of Monroe and DiMaggio's marriage is announced. After the closing events, Grady decides that he needs to commit himself to Sara and to the baby that she is carrying. From the balcony of the college auditorium, he tosses his last bag of marijuana to the janitor. Suffering from yet another of the dizzy spells that have plagued him in past months, he is saved from plummeting to the ground by Sara's sudden appearance and her firm grip. Grady wakes up a few hours later in the hospital; fortified with intravenous fluids and antibiotics for his infected ankle, he checks himself out of the hospital and makes his way to the Gaskell house with tuba in tow. In Sara's greenhouse, he meets "Q" as well as a drunk, angry Walter Gaskell. The latter informs him that he has been suspended and ultimately hits him with a bat that once belonged to Joe DiMaggio. Walking home in the rain, Grady is picked up by Sara.

Narrating in the present and with some temporal distance from that fateful WordFest weekend, Grady teaches creative writing at his alma mater, is writing again after a long hiatus, relishes his son, and can sometimes be found talking with aspiring writers over a beer watered down with lemonade.

CHARACTERS

Grady Tripp, the narrator of the novel, characterizes himself as an "ex-wonder boy" (275). He embodies the dissolute writer who moves from one vice and relationship to another. Averse to commitment and acting

> "I climbed onto Grady's voice and I surfed all the way to the end of the book," says Michael Chabon about the writing of *Wonder Boys*.

like an adolescent despite approaching middle age, he nevertheless strives to control and deflect his lust for his student Hannah Green and struggles with a sense of responsibility to James Leer. Unable to find coherence in his unwieldy epic of the Wonder brothers, he is a tragicomic figure. Both his writing attire—a white chenille bathrobe with geraniums on the pocket—and his close relationship with Crabtree suggest that he is not totally at home with the traditional trappings of masculinity. The possibility of fatherhood becomes a catalyst for Grady's maturation.

Terry Crabtree, like Grady, is an "ex-wonder boy." Alcohol, drugs, and impromptu sexual encounters are the sports of his life. Grady and he underwrite one another's roles as adventurers and philanderers. However, the imminent loss of his editorial position is sobering, and his own past flight from a parental home that deemed homosexuality a sin seems to inspire identification with and tenderness toward James Leer. He is an opportunist but with a heart; his efforts to save James and thus himself provide Grady with an unlikely model to salvage his relationship with Sara.

James Leer has internalized a script of the self-destructive, alienated writer. Mourning the loss of parents and finding himself at odds with an extended familial world of wealth and repression, he has created a persona of an impoverished outcast and rebel and has fixated on Hollywood narratives of suicides. Yet he is also a serious writer who, in sharp contrast to Grady, completes a novel without talking about it. During the weekend chronicled by Grady, James is initiated into the writers' world of alcohol and drugs; he also comes of age sexually. Given the imminent publication of *Love Parade* and his tutelage by Crabtree, James's next performance will be that of an up-and-coming wonder boy, as evidenced by the bow he takes at the last WordFest event. Whether the cycle of the rise and fall of wonder boys will continue with him or be revised remains to be seen.

August Van Zorn and **Joe Fahey** are models of tormented, tragic writers who cannot ultimately sustain a writing life. Van Zorn, the first writer

Grady knew, was plagued by familial tragedy and ultimately committed suicide. Shared knowledge of his obscure writings initiates the friendship of Grady and Crabtree. Notably, James, too, is aware of Van Zorn's writing, which therefore functions as a cross-generational legacy. Joe Fahey is a writer whose success led to his demise. The narratives of these writers' lives haunt Grady.

Antonia/Tony Sloviak cross-dresses and thus intimates that gender is the performance of cultural expectations for behavior and appearance. She/he is treated as a disposable toy by Crabtree; the pathos of this character suggests the consequences of not fitting into preformed gender roles. As Grady watches Antonia transform herself into Tony, he is reminded of the sight of his own father undressing and removing the prosthetic foot that resulted from a war injury.

Sara Gaskell, like many of the male characters, is haunted by the instability of her paternal inheritance: her father had a checkered employment history and choked to death when she was quite young. Although she values pragmatism and rationality, she is an avid and nondiscriminating reader. Even as she wrestles with and is obviously pained by Grady's indecisiveness about the baby she carries, she exudes an aura of competence traditionally associated with masculinity and is profoundly uncomfortable wearing high-heeled shoes, an accessory associated with traditional femininity. Thus, Sara, too, seems to be a gender bender, even as an expectant mother associated with the fertility of her greenhouse.

Emily, Grady's third wife, is a Korean orphan and immigrant. Raised as a Jew in the States by the quirky Warshaws, she strove to conform through apology and concerted efforts to remain unexceptional and thus unnoticed. Although she aspired to be a fiction writer and a mother, she is an ad writer and childless. Her life is sketched as a disappointing one lived on a small canvas, though she does take to the road when she is angry.

Irv Warshaw, Emily's father, still mourns his drowned son, Sam, and is acutely aware that his Jewish family is shrinking rather than growing. Although he is not emotionally expressive, he and Grady are quite fond of one another, and they both keenly feel the potential loss of their relationship due to the dissolution of Grady and Emily's marriage. Irv has constructed a workshop that functions as an adult version of a boys' clubhouse.

Deborah is Emily's sister. In sharp contrast to Emily, she thrives on a life of public drama, and, like Grady, has been married several times. Acutely aware of her own failures and absurdities, she is both protective and disdainful of her sister; her decision to tell Emily about Sara's pregnancy expresses this ambivalence toward her sibling. She is a disruptive force at the seder and appears to flirt with death by ingesting wild mushrooms. Unlike James and Grady, her destructive and self-destructive impulses seem not to be tempered by creative potential.

Peterson Walker, also known as Pea as well as Vernon Hardapple, is the rightful owner of the green Galaxie car that Grady obtained from Happy Blackmore, another unproductive writer. When Grady, Crabtree, and James see him in the Hi-Hat, they treat him as one of their characters and use him as a screen onto which to project their fictions. However, he turns out to have a story of his own that both intersects and radically deviates from their imaginings and expectations. The car originally belonged to Walker's brother, who was murdered, likely in place of his brother. Thus, Walker's history is one of male violence and sacrifice. Grady must do battle with Walker in order to retrieve the stolen Marilyn Monroe jacket from the repossessed Galaxie; that battle is presented ironically as a mythic one, with Grady as the minotaur and Walker as Theseus.

Hannah Green is a Utah native, notable for her self-possession, her red cowboy boots, and her seductive demeanor toward Grady, who is her landlord and creative writing professor. In a reversal of the student-teacher relationship, she recognizes Grady's considerable gifts as a writer, noting with admiration that his sentences seem "as if they've always existed, waiting around up there, in Style Heaven ... for you to fetch them down" (110). She also delivers a painfully accurate critique of his out-of-control, marijuana-induced novel.

THEMES

Through the large cast of writer figures in *Wonder Boys*, Chabon explores the relationship between a writer's life and work. Many writers acquiesce to the romantic model of the alienated, self-destructive writer who sabotages his life in order to provide material for his books. Both Grady and James experience the chaos and angst caused by such a model. Although a writer's experiences, desires, and obsessions are encoded and distilled in the literary work, a writer endangers himself by allowing the line between one's fiction and one's life to become too blurry. At one point, Grady speculates that perhaps Albert Vetch's suicide was the result of living and dying as if he were one of his characters. Another danger is the Keatsian "writing one's life in water" (93), of living one's plots rather than committing them to paper, which is the story of Crabtree's life. The celebrity culture that surrounds writers is also antithetical to the production of literature. Notably, Grady's writing career becomes stalled after he wins a PEN award and is provided an advance for the slightest of ideas. The vacuity of WordFest also depicts literary culture as sometimes hostile to the art of literature. Although conflating literature and life is risky business, our individual and collective lives are shaped, in part, by the narratives we fetishize.

A great deal of narrative time and space in *Wonder Boys* is devoted to a Passover seder, indicating that redemption and liberation are significant themes of the novel. The Passover story tells of the Israelites' flight from slavery in Egypt, a story of freedom meant to be experienced by each generation anew. The Hebrew term for Egypt is *mitzrayim*, literally a narrow place. Significantly, Grady, who has been enslaved by the constant but stultifying work on his novel *Wonder Boys* that he could only do while stoned, is physically trapped in an alley when the pages of his novel fly out of the car. He redeems himself by shedding the literal and figurative baggage he has been carrying and by committing himself to Sara and to his unborn son.

The question of where and to whom one belongs—and why—is another major theme of the novel. The Warshaws' home is located in a town called Kinship that was originally a utopian experiment. Through their adoption of Korean orphans, the Warshaws construct a family, wacky and dysfunctional though it is. Grady, an orphan, seeks a home and family even as he resists such commitments. Van Zorn kills himself in a hotel, a sign that he has only the most provisional home. James Leer, also an orphan, uses his narrative skills to construct an alternative origin story for himself. Terry Crabtree is in exile from his homophobic birth family; despite seemingly relishing the life of a rake, he seeks both refuge with and for James. This theme of belonging is also developed through the lost, stolen, traveling, and returned objects of the book, most notably the green Galaxie and Marilyn Monroe's jacket.

In *Wonder Boys*, Chabon also explores the hidden lives of men. At one point, rummaging through Crabtree's garment bag, he discovers that all his friend's suits are the same and reflects on "Superman's closet at the North Pole, a row of shining suits hanging on vibranium hooks" (72). Men in *Wonder Boys* seem to be in costumes that consign them to different Fortresses of Solitude.

DISCUSSION QUESTIONS

- What are the dramas, challenges, and satisfactions associated with living the life of a "wonder boy" in this novel? Is there a comparable narrative for a "wonder girl"?
- The Passover seder at the Warshaws' is a significant part of the narrative. What is its function in terms of plot, character development, and theme?
- What does Grady's relationship with both James Leer and Hannah Green suggest about relationships between students and teachers?

5

THE AMAZING ADVENTURES OF
KAVALIER AND CLAY
(2000)

The Amazing Adventures of Kavalier and Clay is the tale of two Jewish wonder boys who, in the tradition of Superman cocreators Joe Shuster and Jerome Siegel, give birth to the Escapist, a comic book superhero whose adventures include the winning of World War II. This epic novel, which ranges from Prague in the 1930s to the United States of the 1950s, won a Pulitzer Prize and established Michael Chabon as one of contemporary literature's most distinguished writers. Page numbers cited from *The Amazing Adventures of Kavalier and Clay* are from the 2000 hardback edition (New York: Random House).

NARRATIVE SUMMARY

In Part I, "The Escape Artist," the third-person narrator provides a retrospective on the origin story Sammy Clay tells about his comic book career and then quickly moves to "the true history of the Escapist's birth," beginning with Joe Kavalier's arrival in Brooklyn in 1939. Exhausted and ill from his escape from Nazi-occupied Prague via Lithuania, Japan, and San Francisco, Joe shows up at his aunt's New York apartment with a stack of newspapers, hoping to glean news about the family he left behind. He is eager for work as an artist so that he can earn money to rescue his kin. Sharing a bed with Sammy and a cigarette rolled from the butts of others, Joe becomes Sammy's creative partner.

Joe's life in and escape from Prague is described through flashback. Joe trained for a time with the illusionist Bernard Kornblum. In trying to earn access to the famed Hofzinser Club where the magicians of Prague congregated, Joe attempts a Houdini-esque escape from a sack in the Moldau River. If not for the timely intervention of Kornblum, he and his younger brother, Thomas, would have drowned. When the Nazis invade Czechoslovakia, Joe's family sells everything they own to get him out of Prague; however, a last-minute change of visa rules prevents him from crossing the border. Kornblum, charged with efforts to smuggle the Golem, a legendary clay figure animated through ritual incantations, out of Prague, arranges for his ex-student to stow away in the coffin that contains the Golem's remains. After a harrowing journey, Joe arrives in neutral Lithuania and from there finds his way to the Klaymans' Brooklyn apartment.

At the outset of Part II, "A Couple of Boy Geniuses," Sammy realizes that Joe can draw and decides that they will make money from comic books, a "mongrel art form" (75) whose history is provided by the narrator. They go to the offices of Sheldon Anapol, Sammy's boss and the owner of Empire Novelty Company; there, Sammy proposes that he and Joe develop a Superman-like figure for a comic book series that would contain ads for Anapol's novelties. In the waiting room, Joe draws a picture of the Golem as his first vision of a superhero. Although that vision is deemed too Jewish, Anapol provisionally greenlights Sammy's plan.

As Joe and Sammy brainstorm ideas for their superhero, it becomes clear that a distinctive creation requires a clear and compelling motivation for undertaking the fight against evil. Walking and talking, they meet Julius Glovsky, the brother of Jerry Glovsky, an artist, and head toward the Rathole, the apartment where Jerry and his ethnic artist friends live. Sammy introduces Joe as his partner. Sammy's wish for such a companion had been strong ever since his father abandoned him a second time in 1935 after promising not to do so and news of his death reached the Klayman household a few years later. When they reach the Rathole, Jerry is not there. Joe uses the fire escape to enter the apartment and unwittingly disturbs the nap of a naked Rosa Saks, who flees, but not before Joe gets a good enough look at her to be smitten and to be able to draw her from memory for Julius Glovsky.

In conversation, Joe and Sammy create the Escapist, a superhero whose emblem is a Golden Key passed from generation to generation in the fight against those who represent the Iron Chain. In this generation, the League of the Golden Key must fight the Nazis, and Tom Mayflower, an orphan with a limp, inherits from his uncle Max the "debt" of freedom "that could be repaid only by purchasing the freedom of others" (131). After a weekend of intense work in the Rathole on the Escapist and other narratives, Joe and Sammy present their work to Anapol, who likes it but betrays Sammy by assigning George Deasey rather than Sammy himself to edit the comic book series. Anapol buys the rights to these comic book creations and hires both Sam and Joe for the enterprise; however, he balks at a cover in which the Escapist punches Hitler in the jaw. Joe is invested in that cover for both artistic and emotional reasons. Thus "A Couple of Boy Geniuses" ends with a comic-book-style cliffhanger, in which Joe and Sammy are poised to sell their creations elsewhere if the cover is not approved.

Part III, "The Funny-Book War," opens with the Escapist winning World War II in October 1940, Hitler appearing before a world tribunal, and the Jews of Europe liberated, including, of course, the Kavalier family. However, the news out of Europe and the sporadic, censored letters that he receives from his family remind Joe that his fantasies of liberation, although emotionally, aesthetically, and economically successful, cannot save the Kavaliers. His efforts to bring his family to America have come to naught due to the machinations of the German Consulate as well as the paucity of U.S. visas being issued, despite the threat of genocide. When Joe learns that his father has died, his first impulse is to join the Canadian Royal Air Force to literalize his fighting of the war; however, he decides that he can ultimately be more useful to his family by redoubling his efforts to bring his brother Thomas to the States.

Joe's rage at his father's death and at his own powerlessness takes the form of instigating fights with German Americans, some of whom are antifascist but others who organized out of pride in and support of the Third Reich. Breaking into the offices of the Aryan-American League, single-handedly run by Carl Ebling, he discovers to his great shame that this Nazi sympathizer is a fan of the Escapist. When Ebling surprises Joe by walking into the office, the cocreator of the Escapist wins the ensuing fight. In retaliation, Ebling makes a faux bomb threat to the offices of Empire Comics, now housed in the Empire State Building. Joe, intent on continuing his work and suspecting that Ebling is behind the threat, handcuffs himself to his desk and refuses to evacuate. In this way, Joe earns the attention of Al Smith, chief executive of the corporation responsible for the iconic New York building, and James Haworth Love, an industrialist who decides to sponsor a radio program devoted to the adventures of the Escapist.

Deasey alerts Sammy and Joe that they have no legal rights to profits from a radio program, and that they need to become more savvy about protecting their own economic interests in their creations. That same night, Deasey takes them to an avant-garde party in Greenwich Village hosted by Siegfried Saks, also known as Longman Harkoo. There, Joe saves Salvador Dali from asphyxiating during a performance act gone awry and formally meets Rosa Saks, Siegfried's daughter and the naked woman Joe glimpsed in Julius Glovsky's apartment. Rosa, too, is an artist, obsessed by moths. At the same party, Sammy spies two men kissing and, for the first time, has a vision of gay love that is romantic.

Through Rosa's work at the Transatlantic Rescue Agency, Joe arranges to pay for his brother Thomas and two other children's passage to America on a ship named the *Ark of Miriam*. Influenced by his developing romantic relationship with Rosa, Joe creates the female superhero and sex object Luna Moth, whose alter ego is librarian Judy Dark. Sammy and Joe use this new creation to negotiate with Anapol about profits from the Escapist radio program. Anapol, unnerved by the bomb threat, wants the Escapist to stop fighting the Nazis. Deasey, once again playing advisor to Sammy and Joe, informs them that those who own the rights to Superman are legally pursuing his imitators, including the copyright owners of the Escapist, Anapol and his brother-in-law, Jack Ashkenazy. This information provides Joe and Sammy with much-needed bargaining power.

Part IV, "The Golden Age," begins with an accounting of the economic success of Kavalier and Clay in 1941 and Sammy's meeting of the radio voice of the Escapist, Tracy Bacon, with whom he falls in love, shares an electric kiss atop the Empire State Building, and experiences an intimate evening amongst the remnants of the 1939 World's Fair. Joe occasionally transforms himself into the Amazing Cavalieri, a magician and illusionist for bar mitzvah parties. He trains at Louis Tannen's Magic Shop and begins to believe that his brother, Thomas, will soon be like the boys he entertains, "boys who lived free of the fear of invasion, occupation, cruel and arbitrary laws" (317). At one of these parties, Carl Ebling, working as a waiter, plants a bomb: he wants Jewish boys in New York to get a taste of what their brethren abroad are experiencing. Joe's quick actions prevent Ebling's hate from turning into a tragedy. However, in the chaos that ensues, he loses the last—and unread—letter from his mother. Seeing Orson Welles's *Citizen Kane* inspires Sammy and Joe to take the art of comics to a new level, and the sale of the Escapist to Parnassus Pictures becomes the catalyst for Joe and Sammy to stop aesthetically fighting Nazis and to turn their artistic attention to "the everyday heroics of the 'powerless'" (368).

Thomas's departure on the *Ark of Miriam* is delayed by the anti-Semitic machinations of Breckinridge Long at the State Department, but intervention from Eleanor Roosevelt, with whom Siegfried Saks has a slight acquaintance, soon gets the ship on its way. However, it comes under attack by a German U-boat and, although those on board are successfully removed to lifeboats, a storm causes all to perish at sea. Joe learns about the tragic demise of his brother during a performance of the Amazing Cavalieri at the Hotel Trevi. He agrees to an escape from a wooden packing crate in a fountain, but out of grief, he does not try to liberate himself and is enraged when his suicide attempt fails. That same night, Sammy and Tracy Bacon are caught up in a police raid on the gay haven that is James Love's beach house. Sammy is raped by a federal agent and probably would have been killed had his mother not called to tell him about Thomas's death. Not wanting to "be punished for loving" (420), Sammy decides not to go to California with Tracy. In rage and grief, Joe enlists in the navy to fight the Germans, leaving behind Rosa, who, unbeknownst to him, is pregnant.

Part V, "Radioman," chronicles Joe's time in the navy. Stationed in Antarctica at the Kelvinator Station, Joe is part of a team keeping track of German operations in the polar region. When the stove malfunctions one night while Joe is on guard duty, the altered breathing of Oyster, one of the team's dogs, alerts Joe to the poisonous gas that has already killed all but one man in the unit. Joe and Shannenhouse, a pilot, cannot expect help to arrive until the first thaw several months away. When Joe determines from radio transmissions that a German scientist is in range, he and Shannenhouse prepare the plane for flight; these preparations include the sacrificing of Oyster, Joe's canine rescuer, for his skin. En route to the German installation, Shannenhouse dies of a ruptured appendix; thus, Joe becomes the lone survivor not only of his Czech birth family but also of his unit. Almost mad with grief and rage, Joe savors the prospect of achieving catharsis through the killing of a German. However, as soon as Joe returns fire and hits the German geologist, Mecklenburg, he regrets that he "had allied himself with the Ice" (465). The death of this man who was also caught up in the insanity of war adds to rather than ameliorates Joe's grief.

Part VI, "The League of the Golden Key," begins in Bloomtown at the Clay household, a family established by the marriage of Sammy and Rosa and the birth of Tommy, the genetic progeny of Rosa and Joe named after Thomas Kavalier and legally adopted by Sammy. After Joe left, Sammy struggled professionally; he now writes the storylines for a comic book series that Rosa illustrates. This partnership with Sammy is the remnant of Rosa's artistic career, and it saves her from despair at the loss of Joe and the discontent she experiences as a suburban housewife. Unbeknownst to Sammy and Rosa, Joe has returned to New York and is holed up in an office in the Empire State Building. Having made contact with Joe through Tannen's Magic Shop, Tommy comes up with a scheme to bring Joe back to his parents. His plan entails the announcement of the return of the Escapist in a daring leap from the Empire State Building. Joe is loath to disappoint Tommy, so he dons Tracy Bacon's old Escapist costume, which he steals from the offices of Empire Comics, constructs a flexible bungee cord from rubber bands, and leaps. His makeshift suspension line snaps; luckily, he lands on a ledge and his injuries are not life threatening. This stunt introduces him to the Clay household, and his presence necessarily reconfigures it as he and Rosa are still in love and Joe's identity as another father is revealed to Tommy.

Shortly after Joe's return, Sammy is called to appear before the Senate Subcommittee to Investigate Juvenile Delinquency, which, under the influence of writer/psychiatrist Fredric Wertham, considers comic books to be a moral pollutant. When these hearings result in the public outing of Sammy, Deasey appears once more and suggests that, rather than a tragedy, this development is an accidental proffering of the golden key of liberation.

A heavy wooden crate arrives at the Clay residence containing the remains of the Golem. During Joe's solitary years in the Empire State Building, he has memorialized the lost world of his youth through the creation of a graphic novel featuring the Golem of Prague. Using the money that he had accumulated to rescue his family from Europe, Joe buys Empire Comics for Sammy. However, the latter has decided to take the trip that was aborted years ago and heads west for California.

CHARACTERS

Joe Kavalier is a refugee from German-occupied Prague; as the cocreator of the Escapist, he hopes to rescue his family from Hitler's Europe. However, historical forces prevent such "wishful figments" from being realized. As a man, he must learn the limits of violence; as an artist, he

---

"Breakfast in the Wreck" recounts the morning after Sammy's public outing. This short piece of fiction, originally written as a chapter of *Kavalier and Clay* but ultimately not included in the novel, appeared in the Spring 2004 issue of *Virginia Quarterly Review*.

Sammy's Bloomtown house is on Lavoisier Drive, named after the French scientist known as the father of modern chemistry who identified the role of oxygen in the process of combustion. Lavoisier was a victim of the French Revolution's guillotines after a speedy and specious trial. Sammy's address foreshadows his ill-treatment by the Senate Subcommittee.

develops a Jewish vision. His aesthetic partnership with Sammy Clay is intense and productive.

Sammy Clay is a Brooklyn boy abandoned by his father and burdened by a limp resulting from polio. In an attempt to portray himself as more professional and less Jewish, he changes his name from Klayman to Clay. With Joe as his creative partner, his longed-for transformation is imaginatively accomplished when the character they create, Tom Mayflower, becomes the Escapist. Sammy's romance with Tracy Bacon, interrupted by police brutality, and his subsequent marriage to Rosa represent the challenges of gay life in the pre-Stonewall period.

Ethel Klayman is Sammy's mother, whom he experiences as unsupportive. Her lack of nurturing is symbolically and comically conveyed through her notoriously bad cooking. Yet she seems to recognize and accept Sammy's attraction to Tracy even before he does. Moreover, she does her best to provide a refuge for Joe and to comfort him as his—and her—Czech family is extinguished by forces beyond their control.

Rosa Saks is a female artist figure, Joe's love interest, and Sammy's wife. Torn between avant-garde and more conventional narratives for a woman's life, she ultimately finds herself enacting adventures through her comic book illustrations.

Sheldon Anapol owns Empire Novelties, which morphs into Empire Comics due to the work of Kavalier and Clay. Anapol, "an orphan of pogrom and typhus" (80) and a frustrated violinist, transforms himself into a businessman, one who takes advantage of Joe and Sammy. Sammy feels betrayed by this father/mentor figure, and Joe realizes that his aesthetic work on the Escapist is making Anapol rich but is not having the desired effect of liberating the Kavalier family from Hitler's Europe.

Bernard Kornblum, originally from Eastern Europe but living in Prague, is an atheist who nonetheless is an observant Jew. Kornblum trains Joe in the art of Houdini-esque escapology. He saves Joe's life twice, once by rescuing him from the Moldau River, the other by transporting him out of Prague in the Golem's coffin. He wisely counsels Joe to worry less about "what you are escaping *from*" and more about "what you are escaping *to*" (21). Many of Joe's missteps result from his not heeding this sage advice from his mentor.

Thomas Kavalier, Joe's brother, almost drowns in the Moldau River as a result of Joe's botched escape. Later in the novel, as a ship passenger fleeing Hitler's Europe on the *Ark of Miriam*, he drowns. Thus, his life as well as death is marked by liberation and escape plots gone awry. His surrealistic sketch of Houdini in midair accompanies Joe to New York and then to Antarctica, where it remains.

Herr Dr. Emil Kavalier, Joe's father and a distinguished glandular specialist, was herded into a Prague ghetto with the rest of his family by the German occupying forces, where he succumbs to pneumonia. Joe's glib parting words to his father, "see you in the funny papers" (19), turn out to be poignantly accurate, since only in comic books can Hitler be defeated soon enough to rescue the Kavaliers and others like them. At one point, Joe understands that his father's orderly and ethical conduct, even under the most extreme circumstances, will not alter his fate. Shortly after having a vision of his father at the New York harbor, Joe learns of his death.

Frau Dr. Anna Kavalier, Joe's mother, is an eminent psychiatrist. Joe loses her last, unread letter in the chaos caused by Carl Ebling's attack, although the reader of the novel has access to it. Believing that Thomas is safely on his way to the United States, she urges Joe to turn his attention to the future because she understands herself already to be a ghost.

The Golem of Prague is a Jewish legendary figure constructed from clay and brought to life through the power of ritual words. According to legend, he protected ghettoized and victimized Jews but also could be a destructive force, especially to his creators. Thus, he is an emblem for the ways in which one's creations take on a life of their own; notably, Joe's first image of a superhero is that of the Golem. In the novel, the Golem paradoxically needs to be protected from Hitler's minions, yet his coffin is the means of Joe's escape from Nazi-occupied Europe. At the end of the novel, the crate that bears the Golem's remains is delivered to Joe.

Potentially bearing the millions of souls murdered in the Shoah, the Golem weighs a great deal more than he did when he first left Prague in 1939.

George Deasey is a disillusioned editor/writer who, in spite of his cynicism, periodically advises and provides useful inside information to Sammy and Joe as they negotiate with Sheldon Anapol. Unexpectedly, he plays the role of mentor to Sammy. As a counterpoint to Joe, he sees popular art as money-making trash without aesthetic value.

Alter Klayman, aka Mighty Molecule and Professor Alphonse von Clay, is Sammy's wayward, disappointed, and wandering father. A vaudeville showman, Klayman abandoned Ethel and Sammy when the latter was a very young boy. When he returns during Sammy's adolescence, he promises that, when he leaves again, he will take his son with him. However, Klayman reneges on this promise and abandons Sammy a second time, leaving his son bereft of a father and a male partner. Literally crushed to death by a tractor, he is a case study of American Disillusionment, the title that Sammy gives to the novel that he is perpetually writing.

The Escapist is the Superman-like character that Joe and Sammy create. A limping orphan, Tom Mayflower, is transformed into the Escapist when he receives the Golden Key. Initially, Joe imagines him only as the rescuer of Europe's Jews and the winner of World War II. However, when he realizes that Carl Ebling is a fan of the Escapist, he worries that his and Sammy's antifascist creation might be complicit with a fascist ideology of masculine violence and domination.

Herr Milde is a sadistic German Consulate official whom Joe is forced to deal with as he fruitlessly strives to secure the safety of his Prague family. During a round of the cat and mouse game they play, Herr Milde offhandedly informs Joe that his father is dead. Milde is a petty bureaucrat who nevertheless exposes Joe's powerlessness.

Carl Ebling is the man behind the Aryan-American League. When Joe breaks into the League's office in Yorkville, he discovers that Ebling is a fan of the Escapist, despite his avowed disdain for "Jew cartoonists" (202). Joe bests Ebling in the physical fight that ensues at the office and leaves him a note signed "The Escapist." Ebling is behind the faux bomb threat directed against Empire Comics. More dangerously, acting as the Saboteur, a comic book antagonist of his own creation, Ebling rigs a bomb at a bar mitzah party where Joe is performing his magic act as the

Amazing Cavalieri. Joe's quick action saves the Jewish guests at this function. The politics of World War II are played out domestically between Joe and Ebling as life imitates art.

James Haworth Love is a gay industrial magnate whose politics are anti-fascist, in part because a beloved friend was imprisoned on moral depravity charges and died in Dachau. He is present at the Empire Comics office when Carl Ebling's bomb scare occurs. To support his business interests as well as the anti-Nazi exploits of Kavalier and Clay's superhero, Love provides the brainstorm and the capital for putting the Escapist on radio. Thus, he indirectly enables Tracy Bacon to become the voice of the Escapist. Until it is raided, Love's beach house functions as a rare safe space for gay men, including Sammy and Tracy.

Siegfried Saks, aka Longman Harkoo, is Rosa's father and a well-connected member of the avant-garde. At a party hosted by him, Joe officially meets Rosa, and Sammy gets his first glimpse of gay love. Although Siegfried seeks to welcome Joe into the Saks clan, such welcoming becomes a poignant reminder of the Czech family that Joe has left behind.

Salvador Dali is a famous surrealist painter; in the novel, Chabon imagines that Joe saves this historical figure's life. In that scene, Joe is a rescuer and a guardian of life, in sharp contrast to the role that he plays with the German scientist Mecklenburg.

Herman Hoffman is the Jewish American man who founded the Transatlantic Rescue Agency and is outfitting the *Ark of Miriam* to rescue as many Jewish children from Hitler's Europe as possible. The impediments to this mission and its ultimate tragic failure represent the lack of safe havens for European Jews during the Shoah. In the Bible, Miriam, Moses' sister, is associated with the celebration of the safe passage through the Red Sea and with life-sustaining wells in the desert. Here, Miriam's song of liberation becomes instead a death knell.

Luna Moth, aka Judy Dark, is the fictional librarian transformed into a well-endowed, sexy female superhero. Joe creates this "woman warrior" (272) character in homage to Rosa. Notably, in a reversal of roles, Luna's actions and powers result in the saving of a police officer.

Tracy Bacon is the actor tapped to be the radio voice of the Escapist. As his last name suggests, he is not Jewish, and he is presented as a masculine counterpoint to Sammy. Both of them are lonely and are in the process of coming out. They become lovers and are poised to go together to California where Tracy will be playing the Escapist on screen and Sammy might have the opportunity to write scripts. However, the police raid at Love's beach house dissuades Sammy from making a life with his male lover. Tracy then goes to California without Sammy and ends up dying in World War II when his bomber, aptly named the Liberator, is shot down. After Sammy is outed by the Senate Subcommittee to Investigate Juvenile Delinquency, he regrets forsaking his life with Tracy for the imprisoning security associated with heterosexual marriage.

Ruth Ebling is the sister of Carl Ebling and the housekeeper at James Haworth Love's beach house. When Sammy, the cocreator of the Escapist, shows up at Love's party, her anti-Semitism and homophobia merge with her resentment about her brother's jail sentence for the bar mitzvah bombing. She is the one to call the police and thus initiate the raid.

John Pye is one of the guests at Love's house when it is raided. Having previously endured such raids, he resists this time. Before he is subdued, he destroys a photographer's camera and thus saves the reputations of many of those at the party. He circumvents the U.S. Army's ban on homosexuals and dies serving in World War II.

Agent Wyche is an FBI agent involved in the raid on Love's gay haven. Wyche rapes Sammy, an act that forges a connection between violent homophobia and repressed homoeroticism.

Shannenhouse is a pilot at Kelvinator Station. He and Joe are the only survivors of the malfunctioning stove that turns the station into a poison gas camp and a tomb. Shannenhouse uses the skins of the dogs, including the beloved Oyster, to outfit his plane for the mission against the German base in Antarctica. He dies en route, leaving Joe as the sole survivor of the station and alone on the mission.

Oyster is the dog whom Joe befriends at Kelvinator Station. The dog's altered breathing saves Joe's life by alerting him to the danger of the poison gas; concomitantly, Joe carries Oyster outside to safety, only to later sacrifice him in order to finally see combat with a German. Joe's "betrayed love of Oyster" recalls his relationship with Rosa.

Klaus Mecklenburg is a German geologist who forgoes his peaceful and scholarly inclinations and shoots at Joe as soon as the latter arrives at the German base. Moreover, Mecklenburg misinterprets Joe's decision to throw away his own gun as an act of aggression; throwing himself at Joe, Mecklenburg ends up being shot. Joe tries to save him, but to no avail. Mecklenburg's death causes Joe to regret allying himself with the Ice and death.

Tommy Clay is Rosa and Joe's biological child and Sammy's adopted son. Like both of his fathers, Tommy is obsessed with comic books and has constructed an alter ego for himself in a character of his own creation called the Bug. Although Joe is unable to save his own father, Tommy succeeds in rescuing Joe from his self-imposed exile in the Empire State Building.

Detective Lieber is the detective who investigates the Escapist's return and thus Joe's leap from the Empire State Building. As a Jewish detective, he is charting new ground post–World War II. He and Sammy are attracted to one another and arrange to have lunch, a pattern for the occasional gay tryst that has marked Sammy's marriage to Rosa.

THEMES

The irrecoverable losses of the Holocaust constitute a major theme of the novel. The confirmed deaths of Joe's father and brother, the last letter from his mother that remains unread, and the Golem weighted down with the souls of those who perished in the Shoah represent the development of this theme. The novel also explores the role of art as a means of escape from and memorializing of such grievous loss, while remaining mindful that the "wishful figments" (145) of imaginative work are distinct from the historical record.

The connections and ruptures between the world of European and American Jewry are also represented, especially in the comparative life narratives of Thomas Kavalier and Tommy Clay. *Kavalier and Clay* shows that anti-Semitic terror is contained in the United States, unlike in Nazi-occupied Europe. Anti-Semitism in the United States is represented by Carl Ebling and the State Department. The novel also documents that U.S. Jews assumed leadership in the emerging comic book industry because anti-Semitic employment discrimination prevented them from getting other work as commercial artists.

Intimate family relations—between fathers and sons and between lovers, both gay and straight—are sensitively and poignantly portrayed. Indeed, by providing Tommy Clay with not one but two fathers,

Chabon's research for *Kavalier and Clay* revealed that Orson Welles's *Citizen Kane* influenced a number of legendary comic book artists. Thus, Chabon depicts Joe and Sammy as inspired by the renowned film and has Welles pay a brief but potent compliment to Sammy in the novel: "Great stuff, the Escapist" (358).

Chabon's novel addresses the very definition of family. Relatedly, *Kavalier and Clay* depicts the challenges and possibilities of gay life before the Stonewall riots, an historic marker of the contemporary gay liberation movement. In Joe and Sammy's relationship, Chabon charts the friendship and partnership that can occur between men. Through Joe's fighting World War II in the funny papers, on the streets of Yorkville, and in Antarctica, the novel explores the pattern and perils of masculine violence.

The Amazing Adventures of Kavalier and Clay depicts the aesthetic and political history of comic books. The theme of transformation, a hallmark of the world of superheroes, is woven throughout the text. The artistic value and seriousness of popular cultural forms, which tend toward escapism, is also debated within the pages of this fun yet weighty novel.

DISCUSSION QUESTIONS

- What forms of escape and escapism are at issue in this novel?
- Many historic figures appear in this work. How does such mingling of fiction and history affect your reading of the novel?
- Compare and contrast the development of Joe and Rosa's relationship with that of Sammy and Tracy. What forces help to determine the course of those relationships?
- With which character do you identify the most? Why?

6

THE YIDDISH POLICEMEN'S UNION
(2007)

Set in Sitka, Alaska, and its environs, with Yiddish as the lingua franca, Michael Chabon's *The Yiddish Policemen's Union* is an alternative history of the Jewish people in the twentieth century. What if the United States had, even provisionally, allowed Jewish refugees from Nazi-controlled Europe to settle in its territories? What if the Jewish state of Israel had been demolished in 1948? Chabon presents this alternative history—and alternative present—in the form of a hard-boiled detective story. Page numbers cited from *The Yiddish Policemen's Union* are from the 2008 paperback edition (New York: Harper Perennial).

NARRATIVE SUMMARY

Living in the Hotel Zamenhof, Detective Meyer Landsman is called to investigate the murder of another occupant of the fleabag hotel, a chess-playing heroin addict living under the assumed name of Emmanuel Lasker, a dead author of books about strategic chess moves. Landsman's investigation into this murder is complicated by his messy personal life: alcohol abuse, a divorce resulting from grief and guilt associated with an aborted fetus at risk for a significant birth defect, and the untimely death of his younger sister who was killed when the plane she was piloting smashed into a mountain. Also complicating the investigation is the current political situation: the Federal District of Sitka, established sixty years before as a provisional Jewish homeland for refugees from Hitler's Europe and from the military demise of Israel in 1948, is about to "revert" to U.S. control. Hence most of Sitka's Jews will have to find other places to live as they are, once again, being exiled from the only place they call home. In short, "these are strange times to be a Jew" (7).

Landsman's partner is his cousin Berko Shemets, who is half-Jewish and half-Tlingit, an indigenous Alaskan tribe. Berko spent part of his youth in Meyer's house after his Tlingit mother was killed in rioting that occurred between Jews and native Alaskans. Thus the two men share not only police work but also an intense family history that includes the suicide of Landsman's survivor father and the public scandal surrounding Berko's father, a corrupt counterintelligence agent. Unlike the secular Landsman, Berko is an observant Jew. Early in the novel, Berko's wife, Ester-Malke Taytsh, discovers that she is pregnant with their third child. This news provokes ambivalence since their living quarters are already crowded; moreover, their residency and Berko's employment are uncertain due to the imminence of reversion. On the morning after the murder, Landsman and Berko arrive at Sitka Central to find that Bina Gelbfish, Landsman's ex-wife, is the new inspector of their division for the transition period. Carrying out orders from U.S. agencies, she instructs them in the new policy of "effective resolution": they must close as many cases as possible and bury the ones that seem insoluble, starting with the murder of the Zamenhof junkie.

However, Landsman is not inclined to let go of the case that found him where he lives. Given that the murder victim was a chess player and used the leather straps of tefillin, or phylacteries, to tie off his veins for the injection of heroin, the officially nonexistent murder investigation takes Landsman and Berko first to the Einstein chess club, where Jews from diverse sects weep when they hear about the death of "Emmanuel Lasker." That response leads the detectives to the island of the Verbovers, an ultra-Orthodox sect known not only for its piety but also for the political clout and corruption of its leaders. There, they visit Itzak Zimbalist, who is responsible for maintaining the eruv, or regional boundary, that enables observant Jews to carry items on the Sabbath and holidays without violating religious commandments.

With great and unwonted emotion, Zimbalist identifies "Lasker" as Mendel Shpilman, the son of Verbover Rebbe Heskel Shpilman. Mendel was known as Tzaddik Ha-Dor, the righteous one of his generation with the potential to be the messianic redeemer of the world. In his youth, Mendel was a brilliant scholar and chess player; he also had a gift for bestowing blessings that brought with them miraculous results such as the eradication of cancer in Zimbalist's mistress when she seemed to be on her deathbed. Despite resistance from Rebbe Shpilman's assistant and lawyer, Rabbi Baronshteyn, Berko and Landsman visit the Rebbe right before sundown on the Sabbath. The Verbover Rebbe, notable for his monstrous size as a result of a glandular condition, positively identifies a picture of the murder victim as his son. Shpilman also informs Landsman that he said the Mourner's Kaddish for his son twenty-three years earlier when last he saw him.

Although Bina is officially following the "effective resolution" policy at this point, she does not impede Landman's continued investigation into Mendel's murder. On a tip from a trusted informant on another case, Landsman finds himself in the middle of a gun battle without backup. He ends up killing two wanted suspects and almost dies; however, another suspect, who steals his cell phone and unthinkingly answers it, enables Bina to rescue her ex-husband. He recuperates from his wounds in Berko's home. This incident, coupled with complaints from the Verbovers, causes Landsman to be suspended. That fact does not stop Landsman from pursuing leads in the Mendel Shpilman case.

Landsman's unofficial inquiry takes him to Mendel's funeral and to the limousine that carries Mendel's mother, Batsheva Shpilman. In accordance with her husband, she initially says that she has not seen Mendel for more than twenty years. Yet she shares with Landsman the story of Mendel's break with the Verbovers and the subsequent, sporadic contact she had with him in the intervening years. Despite knowing that her son was gay and that no bride would ever truly be suitable for Mendel, she set up a match between him and an accomplished daughter of a renowned rabbi. On the day of his wedding, Mendel disappeared; however, dressed in widow's garb, Mendel visited his mother to say goodbye and to let her know that he was staying with an old friend. Although her response was one of rejection, which she regretted immediately, he left her with a piece of string, indicating that she would be able to keep in touch with him through Zimbalist, the boundary maven whose medium is string and rope. She provides Landsman with a crucial clue: the last time she spoke with Mendel, she heard loudspeakers in the background, and he had just consumed a piece of pie. Such details place him in the District of Sitka's Yakovy airport, renowned for its pie shop. Notably, this last conversation between mother and son occurred on "the last full day of his sister's life" (227). Thus Mendel's murder and Naomi's death become linked. When Mrs. Shpilman drops Landsman off at the Hotel Zamenhof, she reveals that she confided in him on the recommendation of Bina, who had helped some abused Verbover women years before.

In an interview with the daughter of the airport's pie shop owner, Landsman learns that Naomi had flown Mendel, whom she called "Frank," to Yakovy and asked the daughter to drive him to a nearby motel; he bestowed his blessing upon this formerly troubled young woman. When Landsman investigates the flight plans of Naomi's last days, he discovers irregularities with the FAA files that suggest governmentally sanctioned foul play. In an attempt to learn about Mendel's murder and Naomi's death, he engages the services of a renegade pilot and flies to Peril Strait, where he discovers the Beth Tikkun Retreat Center, a Jewish clinic for substance abuse treatment out of place in non-Jewish territory. Baronshteyn, who appears after Landsman is gun-whipped, makes clear that Landsman is an unwelcome visitor here. Another arrival at the clinic—a powerful American who dislikes messes—delays Landsman's murder. Landsman finds himself drugged and in a cell that once held his sister (her handwriting is literally on the wall).

In an action-packed escape scene, Landsman, wearing nothing but underwear, hurtles himself and the cot to which he is chained through a window and into the snow. He is rescued by Willie Dick, a vertically challenged Tlingit detective inspector. Landsman is arrested by Dick, treated at a hospital for his wounds and hypothermia, and then released into Berko's custody. Berko and Willie know one another from their youth, and despite official impediments, these three policemen strive to untangle the goings on at the Retreat Center. They discover a disguised red heifer, the sacrifice of which is supposed to attend the restoration of the Temple in Jerusalem. Since the Retreat Center would not be allowed to operate in Native Lands without the approval of the U.S. government, the next stop in the investigation is the home of the discredited counterintelligence agent, Hertz Shemets, uncle to Landsman and father to Berko.

Hertz is a ruined man, thanks to the exposé that reporter Dennis Brennan wrote about him. This agent turned hermit devoted his illicit activities toward the goal of permanent status for a Jewish homeland in Alaska; thus, the imminence of reversion is an especially painful prospect for him.

The original title of *The Yiddish Policemen's Union* was *Hatzeplatz*, a Yiddish word that Chabon glosses in the novel as "the back half acre of nowhere" (239). When asked via e-mail about the shift in title, he replied that "the fact that nobody could remember, pronounce, or understand [*Hatzeplatz*] seemed to suggest it might not be a very good title."

When Berko and Landsman provide Hertz with the details of their discoveries thus far, he indicates that Alter Litvak—who worked for him, then betrayed him to Brennan, and who Landsman retrospectively realizes was a shadowy presence at Peril Strait—is a demolitions expert. In order for the Temple to be rebuilt, the Dome of the Rock, Qubbat As-Sakhrah, would have to be removed; Litvak would be a likely man for that job. Hertz also provides details about his work toward permanent status. These activities included orchestrating the bombing of a synagogue in disputed territory that led to the rioting that killed Berko's Tlingit mother, Laurie Jo Bear. Realizing that his father's political activities indirectly took his mother from him, Berko becomes enraged and emotional. He rips off the religious garments that he has worn as a sign of belonging and fealty to his father and winds them around Hertz's face. When Berko and Landsman leave Hertz's home, they hear a gunshot: Hertz has attempted suicide but has botched the job. They rush him to a hospital. Following the phone directive of Ester-Malke, Berko stays with Hertz, while Landsman goes off to find Litvak and avert a plot destined to initiate political turmoil in the Middle East and perhaps World War III.

Landsman reports the findings of his unofficial investigation to Bina, who follows protocol and provides a report to the office of the U.S. Attorney. Mr. Spade, the U.S. official responsible for overseeing the transition, arrives and orders Bina and Landsman to end this investigation; orders to that effect also arrive from the U.S. Attorney's office. However, Bina is now determined to act as a responsible detective and thus disobeys orders. She and Landsman go to the Moriah Institute, run by a Jerusalem-bound dentist named Buchbinder. There they catch up with Litvak, who tells them in writing (his voicebox has been compromised in an accident) about his work with Cashdollar, a U.S. government agent and evangelist charged with "fulfilling the divinely inspired mission of the president of America" (339) to restore the Jews to Palestine in order to propel a Christian apocalyptic narrative into being. Although Litvak is a secular Jew, the prospect of reversion and the displacement of Jews once more convinced him to join forces with Cashdollar. Heskel Shpilman, eager for the rebuilding of the Temple and the coming of the Messiah, was nonetheless too fearful about the potential destruction to the Verbover community to cooperate with the evangelical U.S. government's plot; however, Litvak's offer to restore Mendel to his father and to the Verbovers changed Rebbe Shpilman's mind. Mendel, exhausted from his life as a junkie, initially agreed to enter the treatment center and to play out his generational role; but upon arriving at Peril Strait and learning of the plots afoot that he would serve, Mendel escaped with the help of Naomi.

As Litvak concludes his narration, Berko arrives, threatening Alter Litvak for the role he played in the metaphorical chess game that claimed his mother's life. The cheers of young religious zealots as they watch television at the Moriah Institute indicate that, despite Mendel's escape and murder, the plot to blow up the Dome of the Rock has been enacted. During the chaos that ensues, Litvak disappears, leaving behind the message that he did not kill Naomi. At this juncture, Americans, including Cashdollar, arrive on the scene.

Landsman is interrogated for 24 hours; Cashdollar assures Landsman that, although his predecessor was behind the demise of Naomi, the government was not responsible for Mendel's death. Professing the belief that Jews must be restored to Israel before the end of time can arrive, Cashdollar expresses willingness to hasten the apocalypse but strives to follow his understanding of Jesus' example in not requiring any more destruction than absolutely necessary. In order to achieve his goals, Cashdollar negotiates a deal with Landsman to not reveal his knowledge of this evangelical government plot. Exhausted and demoralized, Landsman trades his silence for the return of his gun and badge as well as a place for Berko in the Tribal Police force once reversion has been completed. After their separate interrogations, Bina and Meyer meet. Overwrought and ashamed, Landsman not only discloses his deal with Cashdollar but also is poised to tell Bina the secret that poisoned their marriage: their aborted son had no visible deformity. However, his disillusioned ex-wife has her own confession to make: exchanging a vow of silence for Landsman's reinstatement as detective, she, too, made a deal.

Determined to find Litvak, the two of them follow the underground tunnels that refugees from Warsaw built under Sitka "against the likelihood of future annihilation" (380). Finding one of the doors secured with string, Meyer and Bina are led back to Zimbalist, the boundary maven. Suspecting him of having information about Litvak, they agree to first find Mendel's murderer before they force his hand on the Litvak question. As they leave Zimbalist's shop, they witness the Shpilman household preparing for the departure to Jerusalem. However, Batsheva Shpilman has vowed not to leave until Mendel's killer is caught. Landsman and Bina promise her that they will do their job.

That night, Landsman slips into Bina's room in her parents' home, and they make love. Following clues from a game of chess that had been under way both in Mendel's hotel room and in Uncle Hertz's cabin, he and Bina end up at Berko's apartment in order to hear Hertz's exposition and confession. In keeping with the chess principle of zugzwang, the necessity to make a move when no good ones are available, Mendel asked Hertz to kill him with the gun that a famous Jewish world champion chess player had used to commit suicide. Mendel first shot up with an ample dose of heroin; then Hertz finished the job with a bullet. Hertz mistakenly believed that the death of the messianic Mendel would thwart Litvak's and the U.S. government's plot to blow up the Dome of the Rock and to initiate the fight for Jerusalem.

Landsman and Bina leave the hospital together. Landsman belatedly apologizes to Bina for making her abort Django; Bina is aghast and bemused that he has assumed responsibility for this decision. Knowing that their promise to Cashdollar to stay silent violates their shared code of ethics, Bina dials Dennis Brennan's number and hands the phone to Landsman, who tells the hungry reporter, "I have a story for you" (411).

CHARACTERS

Meyer Landsman is a decorated detective on a downward spiral. Divorced, alcoholic, mourning both an aborted son and a younger sister killed in a plane crash, he identifies with the chess-playing junkie murdered in the hotel he provisionally calls home. In Yiddish, Landsman means "countryman": thus his state of dispossession is representative. As an adolescent, he repudiated the game of chess, the sole refuge of his survivor-father who ultimately committed suicide. Hence, like Mendel, he refuses his paternal inheritance. He bears profound—and unwarranted—guilt both for the death of his father and for the terminated pregnancy. Landsman has the distinction of being the only detective to make a case against a Verbover. Despite his notable flaws, his tough talk, and his masculine vulnerabilities (including a fear of the dark), he is a mensch, Yiddish for a man exuding common decency. In his lack of focus on the future, he is a counterpoint to those with messianic yearnings. He redeems himself by upholding his ethical code even when it is unfashionable and politically inexpedient to do so.

Berko Shemets is Landsman's partner and cousin. A physically imposing figure, he is the biological son of Laurie Bear and Hertz Shemets; his mixed parentage caused him grief as a youth but allows him access to both the Tlingit and Verbover worlds as a police detective. He has chosen to be an observant Jew "in his own way and for his own reasons" (41). In sharp contrast to Landsman, he is a stable family man and has two sons. When his mother was killed in politically orchestrated riots, his father left him in the Landsman home. Despite Landsman's instability, Berko is intensely loyal to him and always finds room for him in his cramped home; just as Landsman rescued him as a youth, he now regularly rescues Landsman. Like Landsman, Berko learns family history from the evolving Shpilman murder case: his father, Hertz, bears indirect responsibility for his mother's death and for poisoning relations between the Tlingit and the Jews, thus making Berko a boy/man caught between worlds. This discovery causes an outpouring of grief and rage, checked only by the intervention of his wife and by Landsman's suggestion that Berko is acting as crazy as Landsman himself.

Ester-Malke Taytsh is Berko Shemets's wife and the mother of sons Goldy and Pinky. At the outset of the novel, she is coming to terms with her third pregnancy at a historical moment of insecurity and uncertainty. She is unsentimental, pragmatic, and astute; for example, realizing that Landsman is exhibiting signs of alcohol withdrawal, she provides him with a morning beer along with a waffle. She also strong-arms Berko into staying at his father's side after a botched suicide attempt. Like Queen Esther, her biblical namesake, Ester-Malke plays her role in ensuring Jewish continuity, against all odds.

Naomi Landsman is Meyer's younger sister. She is killed in a plane crash engineered and covered up by the U.S. government because she knew too much about the Peril Strait operation and aided Mendel in escaping from Beth Tikkun. Like Meyer, she is independent, a champion of the underdog, and thus often a vexing figure to those more inclined simply to follow orders. A masculine woman, she is often read as a lesbian, a label which she embraces "in everything but sexual preference" (238). Her fearlessness and sardonic smarts remain with her until the end of her life, as the inscription in her detainment cell demonstrates. Notably, she and Meyer's ex-wife, Bina, constituted a mutual admiration society.

Mendel Shpilman, son of Heskel and Batsheva Shpilman, was a prodigy known as a Tzaddik Ha-Dor, the righteous one of his generation. Some believed that he had messianic capabilities. He certainly had a gift for healing others, though not himself, and was much loved by those with whom he had contact, Verbovers and non-Verbovers. Throughout his young life, he struggled with his being, including his homosexuality. Ultimately, he manipulates his own murder rather than be a pawn for an evangelical U.S. government and Verbover plot to rebuild the Temple in Jerusalem. His great tragedy was that "he didn't want to be what he wasn't, he didn't know how to be what he was" (404). Mendel's gifts are a challenge to the religious skeptics and nonbelievers in the novel, including Landsman.

Django is the "codename" for the male fetus that Bina Gelbish aborted when it was revealed to have a chromosomal abnormality that might result in a serious birth defect. The abortion might be considered a familial version of the zugzwang, a term in chess for the move you make when you have to make one but have no good ones available. The loss of Django creates a rift between Bina and Meyer that results in their divorce. Only at the end of the novel, when Meyer and his ex-wife are reconciled, is Meyer relieved of the guilt, though not the mourning, that he experienced over Django and the familial path not taken.

Bina Gelbfish is an inspector and Landsman's ex-wife. At the outset of the novel, she is appointed to lead Sitka Central through the transition period; thus, much to Landsman's chagrin, she becomes her ex-husband's boss. She is competent, serious about her career and her responsibilities as a police officer, and believes in following orders and policy. However, she also knows how to make use of informal channels and paves the way for Landsman to get access to Batsheva Shpilman in his investigation of Mendel's murder. Moreover, she assumes a lead role in the investigation once it becomes obvious that acquiescence to orders would make her complicit with a wide-scale government conspiracy. Like Landsman, she is ultimately guided by her commitment to menschlichkeit, a code of conduct that places a premium on being a good, decent, and compassionate human being. Bina is characterized by her appetite, her red hair that evades concerted attempts to keep it under control, and her ample breasts, as well as by the leather tote bag in which she seems to carry the world. Landsman credits Jews like her with "the wide range and persistence of the race" (155).

Elijah is the name given to an old itinerant man who appears outside the Hotel Zamenhof after Mendel has been murdered; he is collecting money for L'Eretz Yisroel (the land of Israel). Like his biblical namesake, he announces the coming of the Messiah—but in tones that seem devoid of comfort. Despite himself, Landsman contributes to the old man's charity box; however, when Landsman subsequently responds sardonically to the notion of the imminent messianic age, Elijah returns his donation. This encounter, quite early in the novel, foreshadows Mendel's association with messianic longings and plots and Landsman's aversion to them.

Hertz Shemets is Landsman's uncle and Berko's father. As a member of the FBI, he conducted counterintelligence work for the U.S. government. Using the knowledge and connections associated with that position, he worked tirelessly and corruptly for permanent status for a Jewish homeland in Alaska. Thus, the prospect of reversion as well as Zionist yearnings for a return to Israel were anathema to him. His career was marked by a willingness to engage in unethical tactics, culminating in his acquiescence to Mendel's death wish. He is a failed father/father-figure to Berko and Landsman.

Isidor Landsman is a survivor of the Destruction, as the Holocaust is termed here, but ends up a suicide. Hertz Shemets strives to care for Isidor when they meet again after the war, and Isidor marries Hertz's sister, Freydl. However, Isidor is a shell of a man; obsessed with chess, he tries to compel his son, Meyer, to adopt this game of strategy leading to checkmates, but Meyer rebels. Shortly before Isidor's suicide, Meyer wrote his father a letter repudiating the game; after decades of feeling guilt for his father taking his own life, Meyer discovered that his father never opened the letter. Meyer also remembers Hertz's devastation when Isidor died. Repressed grief as the legacy of the Shoah and as an undercurrent of relations between men becomes attached to the memory of Isidor.

Dennis Brennan is the Gentile journalist who exposed the corrupt career of Hertz Shemets and to whom Bina and Landsman turn to tell the story of the evangelist U.S. government/Verbover plot to blow up the Dome of the Rock and establish the Third Temple in Jerusalem. Brennan is a counterpoint to such Americans as Spade and Cashdollar.

Hershel, the dog, belongs to Mrs. Kalushiner, proprietor of the Vorsht, a club where musicians rather than police officers congregate, and thus where Landsman and Berko take refuge to talk about the unofficial investigation of Mendel's murder. Although Nathan Kalushiner has been dead for five years, his dog, leashed, awaits him expectantly. This sight unsettles Berko, who liberates the dog from his leash and lets him out the front door. However, after a brief absence, the dog returns and waits "patiently for the leash to be restored" (81). This vignette, with its mixture of pathos and humor, functions as commentary on the wait for the messiah.

Alter Litvak worked for Hertz Shemets, betrayed him to Dennis Brennan, and now works for Cashdollar and with the Verbovers, despite his being "a secular warrior" (346). He is a veteran of the Cuban war, and the car accident that killed his wife also robbed him of his voice. In Yiddish, his name means old Litvak, the rational Jewish type associated with Haskalah, the Enlightenment, and opposed to Hasidism. Litvak's encounter with Mendel unsettles his opportunistic, pragmatic, and religiously skeptical approach to the world and politics.

Itzak Zimbalist married a Verbover woman; thus, he is an insider/outsider figure in that world and, appropriately, is the eruv, or boundary maven. His maps of Verbover territory provide him with intimate knowledge, which makes him a useful informant for Landsman and Berko. He was Mendel's chess teacher and aided the young Tzaddik Ha-Dor when the latter chose to leave the Verbovers rather than go through with an arranged marriage. Mendel's blessing cured Itzak's mistress. A hardened operator, Itzak is nonetheless emotionally overwhelmed by the news of Mendel's murder.

Rebbe Heskel Shpilman is Mendel's father and the corrupt leader of the Verbovers. He is monstrously large, the result of a glandular disorder. After the losses of the Holocaust, he rebuilt the Verbover court in the District. Despite his corruption, his eyes are discerning, and Landsman comes to appreciate the source of his power in the black-hatted world. Heskel observes that both Mendel and Landsman have been ill-served by less than admirable fathers; this observation unsettles Landsman as it furthers the identification between him and Mendel. Notably, Rabbi Shpilman initially refused to join Litvak and the Americans in the plan to bomb the Dome of the Rock. Remembering that only eleven Verbovers survived the Shoah, he was loath to take risks with his regenerated community; moreover, he is cognizant that the coming of the messiah must occur according to divine rather than human plan. However, the prospect of his son being rehabilitated and returning to the fold convinces him to join forces with the evangelist American conspiracy.

Batsheva Shpilman is Mendel's mother and the Verbover rebbetzin (rabbi's wife). When Landsman deposits himself unceremoniously in her limousine after Mendel's funeral, she provides him with useful background about Mendel's departure from the Verbovers and her sporadic contact with him. Also during their encounter, she provides commentary on maintaining marital harmony and on the "shortfall" between the ideal and the real known as "the world" (214). Notably, she praises Bina. She also refuses to join the Verbover evacuation to Jerusalem until her son's killer is apprehended; thus, she, a traditional Jewish woman, is in league with members of the secular Yiddish policemen's union.

Rabbi Baronshteyn is a lawyer and Rebbe Shpilman's personal assistant, or *gabay*, whose menacing presence Landsman encounters first in the Verbover rebbe's home and then later at Peril Strait. Landsman initially assumes that Baronshteyn helped to orchestrate or, at least, celebrates Mendel's death, since the demise of the Verbover son leaves room for a substitute "heir apparent" (261). However, Baronshteyn's investment in the sojourn to Jerusalem and the rebuilding of the Temple means that the destruction of Mendel's messianic potential is a real loss.

Dr. Buchbinder, a dentist, is committed to the rebuilding of the Temple and the coming of the messianic age. Although he is referred to as an "archaeologist of delusion," his comment to Landsman that he will soon be going to Jerusalem is an early clue about the plans afoot to blow up the Dome of the Rock and relocate the Verbover court to Israel. Landsman and Bina go to Buchbinder's Moriah Institute to speak with Litvak; there they find a model of Mount Moriah, the site of the binding of Isaac and King Solomon's Temple. When Buchbinder presses a button, a replica of the desired Third Temple arises. Buchbinder's model anticipates and summarizes the desires and plot put into play by Cashdollar and Litvak with Verbover support.

Benito Taganes is the proprietor of Mabuhay ("long live" in Tagalog, a Philippine language) Donuts. His donuts are "a tight paper packet of heaven" (174), the extent of the secular police officers' messianic yearnings. Taganes is also Landsman's most valuable informant. Taganes's lover is Olivia, a transgender woman; Landsman rescued Olivia from and enacted revenge upon the serial rapist that attacked her, thus establishing a lifetime bond between Taganes and Landsman.

The Zilberblat brothers are the protagonists of one of Landsman's open cases. Victor Zilberblat was murdered; his brother, Rafi, is a prime suspect. Landsman pursues a lead that Taganes provides; in the shootout that ensues, Landsman kills Rafi and is shot by another Zilberblat brother, Willie. This case of fraternal strife is both an instance of the violence that often characterizes male-male relations and a counterpoint to the love and loyalty, sardonically expressed as it is, between Landsman and Berko.

Wilfred Dick is a Tlingit detective. As a youth, this literally small man and the large Berko played basketball together, engaging in "the kind of grand romantic hatred that in thirteen-year-old boys is indistinguishable from or the nearest they can get to love" (286). This historic bond contributes to Willie Dick's decision to help Berko and Landsman scout out the grounds around the Peril Strait facility, despite the fact that he has been instructed by his superiors not to make inquiries about Jewish activity in "the Indianer-Lands." "Dick" is a slang term for detective as well as male genitalia; thus, his name alludes to the masculine genre-play at work in the novel.

Spade's name calls to mind Sam Spade, the archetypal hard-boiled detective made famous in Dashiell Hammett's *The Maltese Falcon*.

Mr. Spade is the U.S. official assigned to Sitka Central to oversee the reversion transition. His Yiddish is "wretched but energetic" (325). All in the novel understand his function in the terms of Jewish death rituals: he is a shoymer, a representative of the burial society who sits with the dead body of a Jew until the funeral. Notably, he sports a fish pin on his lapel, which indicates that his governmental function is inextricably related to his Christian evangelical credentials. He politely but assertively tries to shut down the pursuit of Alter Litvak in relation to the investigation of Mendel's murder; in charge of Sitka Central until the reversion actually takes place, Bina successfully reestablishes her authority, moral and otherwise.

Mr. Cashdollar is the high-ranking U.S. government official who does not like messes, whose arrival at Peril Strait prevents the immediate shooting of Landsman, and who coerces Landsman into a promise of silence about the conspiracy that he has uncovered in the course of investigating Mendel Shpilman's murder. Cashdollar, whose American opportunism is embedded in his name, confirms that his predecessor was behind Naomi's death and that the government's religious interest in "fulfilling what is written" (368) is behind its efforts to help Jews rebuild the Temple. Toward the end of the novel, Bina is grieved by the realization that, despite her career and ideals in public service, she—like all of the District's Jews—has been a pawn of Cashdollar and his people.

THEMES

In this novel, Michael Chabon recalls, even as he rewrites, a great deal of Jewish history. While the losses of the Shoah and the founding of Israel resulted in the diminishment of Yiddish and the rebirth of Hebrew, *The Yiddish Policemen's Union* strives to re-create the pre–World War II world of Eastern European Yiddishkeit. In part, this is accomplished through the language of the novel. Literal translations of Yiddishisms often appear. For example, at one point, Litvak writes, "Man makes plans. . . . And God laughs" (95), a translation of "a mentsh tracht und

> In this alternative history, Chabon makes the Jewish death toll of the Destruction two million. By imaginatively saving four million Jews from the gas chambers, Chabon enables the survival and flourishing of Yiddishland in Sitka.

Gott lacht." The phrase "bang me a kettle," used throughout the novel, is the English translation of "hak mir nisht ken tshaynik." Yiddish-English puns also appear. For example, in Yiddish, sholem means "peace"; however, in the novel, it refers to a gun, known as a "piece" in the American slang characteristically used in the detective novel. Similarly, a "shoyfer," the ram's horn blown during the Jewish High Holidays, refers to a phone in the novel.

Jewish history is also conveyed through the geography of Sitka. For example, Max Nordau Street is named after a Hungarian Jew whom anti-Semitism made a practical Zionist and who advocated the development of "muscle Judaism." The Ringelblum Avenue Baths, where Litvak meets with Rebbe Shpilman, are named after the Resistance leader and historian of the Warsaw Ghetto. The Hotel Zamenhof bears the name of the Bialystock-born Jewish linguist who was the founder of Esperanto, a universal language. Yiddish literary history is encoded in the reference to Sholem-Aleykhem Park, named after the writer who penned the Tevye stories on which *Fiddler on the Roof* is loosely based. Asch Street is named after the writer of *The God of Vengeance*, a play that includes a romantic relationship between the daughter of a brothel owner and a prostitute.

In the creation of a provisional Jewish homeland and the imminence of reversion, the novel represents the challenges and fears faced by Jews living in the diaspora and the impact that narratives of exile and a home in Zion have on Jewish psyches. The heterogeneity of the Jewish people is also a major theme, developed especially in the depiction of alliances and tensions between religious and secular Jews. The values of menschlichkeit, literally "acting like a human being," dominate the novel.

The difficulties, joys, and mysteries of heterosexual marital relations are explored most prominently through Landsman and Bina's relationship and romantic history; the depiction of the Taytsh-Shemets home as well as that of the Shpilmans' marriage underscores this theme. Challenges to sexual and gender norms are omnipresent throughout the novel. The loves, hatreds, and ambiguities that mark relations between men, especially fathers and sons, are also palpable in the pages of the novel.

In order to solve cases, detectives must construct a story from existing material and narratives. Thus, detectives in *The Yiddish Policemen's Union* are writer-figures, and storytelling emerges as a major issue. The extent to which we tell stories—about home, identity, religion, politics, and love—or stories tell us is one of the questions that this novel raises but refuses to answer definitively.

DISCUSSION QUESTIONS

- What challenges do the Jews of Sitka face in the novel? How does history contribute to their current situation?
- In what ways is the detective work of Meyer Landsman analogous to the work of a writer?
- What are the tensions and overlaps between religious and secular Jews in the novel? Which characters seem to bridge the gaps between these two groups?

7

TODAY'S ISSUES IN MICHAEL CHABON'S WORK

A variety of factors explain Michael Chabon's popularity. He is a master storyteller, he creates compelling characters, he works in the borderlands between literary and popular fiction, and as he himself realized at a very young age, he and "the English ... language seemed to have something going" (Chabon, "My Back Pages," *Maps and Legends*, 148). However, his work also appeals to readers because it taps into the zeitgeist, the spirit of the times. In particular, his work reflects and shapes contemporary thinking about gender and sexuality issues, especially relations between men. In much of Chabon's fiction, meditations on masculinity relate to questions of Jewish identity and history.

Often, when people hear the word "gender," they automatically think about women's issues. Women are commonly assumed to be gendered beings—that is, cultural ideas and expectations about femininity affect women's lives in diverse ways, directly and indirectly. For example, the idea that women are supposed to become mothers affects whether and how they express ambivalence about that role and how women who choose not to have children are regarded. Contemporary feminist movements and gender studies scholars, however, have increasingly called attention to the ways in which men are also gendered beings. Indeed, dominant cultural ideas about masculinity, often opposed to femininity, profoundly shape men's lives and relationships—with themselves, with women, and with other men.

Gender questions are inevitably linked to those involving sexuality. Stereotypical notions of "real" men erroneously equate masculinity with heterosexuality and homosexuality with femininity. Such sharp divides between masculinity and femininity, heterosexuality and homosexuality create a great deal of policing of the relationships between men. Chabon regards the "absolute poverty of male friendships" to be an American tragedy and thinks that men are wounded by their inability to "express their range of feelings in other than the most limited ways" (quoted in Wilson). In his fiction, he explores the "rich territory" of male-male relationships: "fathers and sons, brothers, best friends, male lovers, whatever the permutations" (quoted in Judy Oppenheimer).

Barack Obama used the first Father's Day of his presidency to hold a national conversation about responsible fatherhood, to advocate for paternal involvement, and to cite, from personal experience and sociological statistics, the "hole in a child's heart" that an absent father leaves. In Chabon's world, fathers and sons long for and often fail one another. In *The Mysteries of Pittsburgh*, Art's father typically treats Art to a fancy dinner when the former has "business" in Pittsburgh; however, these meetings are fraught with tension. The mysterious circumstances surrounding Mrs. Bechstein's death and their inability to talk about their shared longing for her create distance between father and son. Mr. Bechstein's desire to have Art live a protected and respectable life, in sharp contrast to his own, causes him to badger Art about his plans for the summer after college graduation. Mr. Bechstein's interventions indirectly lead to the police chase that ends with Cleveland's death. Notably, Art is physically hurt and emotionally traumatized by these events. Moreover, by trying to break up the relationship between Arthur and Art, Mr. Bechstein ends up causing the severance of his own relationship with Art. Ultimately, Mr. Bechstein's attempts to protect his son fail. Cleveland, too, has a tragic history with his father. Dr. Cleveland Arning's clandestine affairs with men drove Cleveland's mother to suicide. As with Art's family, hidden relations between men destroy a woman, and a father indirectly but literally leaves his son motherless.

In *Wonder Boys*, Grady Tripp's father is a suicide; Meyer Landsman, protagonist of *The Yiddish Policemen's Union*, likewise has a paternal legacy of suicide. In *Kavalier and Clay*, Sammy's father, a circus performer billed as the strongest man, abandons him and then dies in an accident. Meyer is haunted by the sense that his characteristic pessimism determined the abortion of the fetus that, if viable, might have been his son. Mendel Shpilman, also of *The Yiddish Policemen's Union*, orchestrates his murder-suicide because he cannot assume the messianic mantle desired by members of his father's sect and evangelical Christian

Zionists. Although crime literally defines the father-son relationship in Chabon's *The Mysteries of Pittsburgh*, it functions as a metaphor for many of those relationships throughout his body of work.

In "The Binding of Isaac," an essay included in *Manhood for Amateurs*, Chabon expresses his sense that paternal failure is inevitable; such failure is often spectacular in his fiction. Significantly, sons fail their fathers as well. One of the most poignant examples is Joe's parting words to his father, "See you in the funny papers," in *The Amazing Adventures of Kavalier and Clay*. Joe immediately regrets this cavalier instance of masculine bravado; this regret only deepens when it becomes clear that he can only rescue his family and the Jews of Europe from the genocidal machinations of Hitler in his comic book imagination. Indeed, his father dies in the ghetto that Jewish Prague becomes. Ultimately, relations between fathers and sons are not only the stories of individual families but also larger histories of ethnoreligious groups.

Young men bereft of fathers often desperately search for mentors; notably, President Obama urged those who do not become biological fathers to look for opportunities to mentor youth. In keeping with the distance that fathers and sons must travel, Chabon depicts reluctant mentors. Grady Tripp of *Wonder Boys* and his protégé, James Leer, ultimately do their part to rescue one another from destructive self-fulfilling prophecies of writers as despairing and solitary individuals. Nonetheless, early in the novel, Tripp acquiesces to Leer's request to leave him literally in the dark after his creative writing classmates tear apart one of his short stories. In *The Amazing Adventures of Kavalier and Clay*, Deasey provides Sammy with useful guidance on the business of comic books as well as the perspective that Sammy's outing by the Senate subcommittee might be a form of liberation. Yet Deasey works overtime to prevent an ongoing, emotionally intimate relationship from developing. His cynicism, sarcasm, and strict conversational limits—especially on the particulars of Sammy's same-sex relationships—function to keep these men apart.

Although the impediments to male friendship are formidable, they are not insuperable, and Chabon's fictional universe attests to the collaborative, creative possibilities that can occur between men. His two gentlemen of the road, Amram and Zelikman, depend on one another for security and companionship, even though tough talk and even verbal abuse are the means by which they express their affection for one another. The Yiddish policemen Meyer Landsman and Berko Shemets also talk tough with one another. However, the two have grown up together and have a shared history of suicidal and corrupt fathers; notably, Meyer often takes refuge in Shemets's crowded domestic space. The creative partnership between Joe Kavalier and Sammy Clay is fully realized and profoundly productive. They begin by sharing a bed and a smoke; through conversation, they give birth to the Escapist and to their careers as Golden Age comics creators. When Sammy realizes Joe's emotional investment in a controversial cover featuring the Escapist punching out Hitler, he stands by his friend; when Sammy is creatively floundering, Joe overcomes his aversion to using the money that he had saved for his now dead family and buys Empire Comics for Sammy. Like Joe and Sammy, Grady Tripp and Terry Crabtree of *Wonder Boys* have a decades-long partnership. Such close friendships between gay and straight men are noteworthy, since homophobic fear or "homosexual panic," as Eve Kosofsky Sedgwick terms it, often keeps men distant from one another. Chabon, in keeping with contemporary queer theorists and activists, thinks that "there's a paucity of labels for people's sexuality." For him, one of the social functions of fiction is to "fill up the gaps in our vocabulary that allow us so few true options for expressing our feelings about people of the same sex" (Gross, "Writer Michael Chabon").

Traditional heterosexual masculinity distinguishes identification (the feelings that a man has toward those whom he admires and wants to be like; for example, fathers and mentors) from desire (the feelings that a man has toward love interests). In Chabon's fiction, however, desire and identification overlap. For example, *The Mysteries of Pittsburgh*'s Art Bechstein clearly strives to emulate Arthur even as he becomes sexually involved with him. When Sammy Clay and Joe Kavalier are in the process of becoming creative partners, Sammy's feelings for his cousin seem dispersed between the seemingly oppositional poles of identification and desire. During the subcommittee hearings, the censorious senators suggest that Sammy's penchant for creating superheroes with young sidekicks is a function of his homosexual "proclivities" or his desire for intimate relations with men; Sammy views this creative impulse as an expression of his search for a father figure. Chabon's fiction opens a space for such feelings to coexist rather than to be mutually exclusive.

As the subcommittee hearings demonstrate in *The Amazing Adventures of Kavalier and Clay*, Chabon's fiction chronicles not only men's complex yearnings for one another but also the resistance to and difficulties in expanding the norms of masculinity and male-male relationships. In *The Mysteries of Pittsburgh*, Phlox expresses her disgust with homosexuality in a letter to Art that ultimately reaches his father; Mr. Bechstein then does everything in his power to separate Art from Arthur. Art's sexual confusion and angst throughout the novel are magnified by the cultural prescriptions and prohibitions regarding gender and sexuality that both Phlox and Mr. Bechstein represent. Until Sammy

Clay attends a party at the avant-garde home of the Sakses and happens upon two men kissing, he had never imagined that romance could be part of gay love. In *The Yiddish Policemen's Union*, Mendel Shpilman's downfall seems to be that he cannot imagine a way to negotiate his complex spiritual and erotic desires within the parameters of a Verbov communal life or wholly outside it; thus, his messianic possibilities are lost to the world. James Leer, one of the wonder boys in Chabon's novel of that name, is a suicidal pariah until Crabtree expresses interest not only in his writing but also in his body. Silence about and a lack of representation of gay life and diverse male desires constitute a cultural form of the "don't ask, don't tell" policy; Chabon's fiction portrays such social tendencies as the stuff of tragedy.

The debate about gay marriage, headline news all around the country, is ultimately about the cultural legitimacy of gay relationships, an issue Chabon tackles in *The Amazing Adventures of Kavalier and Clay*. Sammy's relationship with Tracy Bacon develops parallel to Joe's relationship with Rosa. However, while Joe and Rosa are publicly acknowledged as a couple and are legally protected, Sammy and Tracy only meet in secluded places and are ultimately victimized by a police raid upon a gay haven. After experiencing such police brutality, Sammy breaks off his relationship with Tracy, marries Rosa, and lives a life that seems to match the title of his unfinished novel, *American Disillusionment*. At the end of *Kavalier and Clay*, Sammy leaves for California where, years before, he had planned to go with Tracy; having been outed, Sammy heads westward, a conventional American journey signifying new possibilities and fortunes.

Michael Chabon's own literary reputation has been impacted by the usually strict boundary between straight and gay identities and communities. After the publication of *The Mysteries of Pittsburgh*, in which first-person narrator Art Bechstein has intimate relations with both Phlox and Arthur, Chabon was assumed to be a gay writer. When Ayelet Waldman, now his wife, read that novel before their first date, she wondered why she was being set up with a gay man. Although Chabon was surprised to be identified by *Newsweek* as a young gay writer, he expresses profound gratitude for the gay readership that has followed his career, and Bahr, writing for *The Advocate*, comments that "it's refreshing to meet someone who views being mistaken for gay as a stroke of luck."

Traditional masculinity encourages stoicism and a heightened sense of individualism, which lends itself to isolation. Such tendencies inhibit not only diverse relationships between men but also men's intimate relations with women. An excessive sense of self-reliance often does great harm to men's psychic and even physical health. When Joe Kavalier's brother drowns, Joe responds by joining the navy. His motivation is not only to fight the Nazis but also to be in flight from Rosa. In his grief, he instinctively retreats rather than seek solace from his female lover. Notably, even when Joe returns to the States, he does not know how to reintegrate himself into any sort of domestic life; rather, he hides in the Empire State Building, his version of Superman's Fortress of Solitude. His plan to reappear in the lives of the Clays involves a potentially self-destructive leap from that iconic building.

Similarly, in *The Yiddish Policemen's Union*, Meyer Landsman's grief and guilt over the aborted fetus takes the form of withdrawal from his wife Bina; they divorce and he ends up residing in a flophouse. Notably, his despair and isolation result in his abuse of alcohol. Substance abuse problems are a pattern among men in Chabon's fictional world. In *The Mysteries of Pittsburgh*, Cleveland is an alcoholic; Grady Tripp and Terry Crabtree of *Wonder Boys* use drugs and alcohol to evade and deal with the challenges of everyday life; Mendel Shpilman, whose dead body is at the center of *The Yiddish Policemen's Union*, is a heroin addict; and Zelikman's opium habit seems both cause and effect of his depressive personality in *Gentlemen of the Road*. Upholding the bravado performances of traditional masculinity appears to require painkillers; indeed, conventionalized notions of manhood seem hazardous to men's health.

Michael Chabon's explorations of masculinity relate to his meditations on Jewish identity. Historically, Jewish men have often been regarded as feminized and weak because they earn status within religious communities through study rather than physical feats of strength, and anti-Semitic thought has often negatively characterized Jews as sexually perverse gender benders. Thus, questions of gender are inextricably but also complexly connected to ethnic and religious identity. Jews sometimes assimilate by conforming to dominant gender definitions; for example, Jewish men might present themselves as studs or fighters in order to be perceived as "real men." However, gender conformity may also be used for Jewish self-assertion, such as when Jewish men physically fight to defend their communities against anti-Semitic attacks. Sometimes gender nonconformity becomes a strategy to resist assimilation and to embrace Jewish difference. Thus, as Jews and as men, Jewish men might express pride in rather than apologize for a tradition of study and non-violence.

In *The Amazing Adventures of Kavalier and Clay*, the use of violence, a traditionally masculine trait and strategy, illustrates well the complex intersections of gender and Jewishness. As Joe experiences himself as more and more powerless to save his family from Hitler's genocidal program, he not only inks the comic book superhero punching out Hitler but also begins to pick fights with German New Yorkers and ransacks the offices of the Aryan-American League. Moreover, when he receives news that a German U-boat has been involved in the sinking of the ship that was carrying his brother to safety, he joins the navy, is stationed in Antarctica, and assumes that killing a German will assuage his grief. However, just as he had begun to wonder whether violent superheroes were perpetuating a culture of masculine violence, he discovers that the killing of a German scientist adds to rather than lessens his mourning. Forgoing violence and turning his attention to memorializing Jewish Prague through his graphic novel provide a measure of healing. Thus, his attempts to assimilate to dominant models of violent masculinity fail him. Indeed, Joe's Jewish manhood is most fully realized when he is drawing rather than fighting. In *Gentlemen of the Road* and *The Yiddish Policemen's Union*, Chabon depicts Jewish men with swords and guns, thus challenging the idea that Jewish men are incapable of fighting. However, even these Jewish tough guys reflect a great deal on the uses and abuses of violence.

Of course, such reflection is consonant with the legacy of the Holocaust, an issue that has become dominant in Chabon's work. As the generation of Holocaust survivors and witnesses ages and dies, many contemporary Jewish writers struggle to address the Holocaust in ways that are historically responsible while still maintaining the creative, imaginative license that is the essence of literature. In *Wonder Boys*, the only short story that Terry Crabtree writes is one about Sherlock Holmes and Hitler. This narrative detail anticipates Chabon's *The Final Solution*, in which Sherlock Holmes's reason is overwhelmed by the irrational violence of attempted genocide. In that work, the most that the great detective can do is to help restore a kidnapped parrot to a young survivor who has lost everything else. *The Amazing Adventures of Kavalier and Clay* also chronicles the losses of the Holocaust as well as the ways in which art can memorialize but not reverse such losses. In *The Yiddish Policemen's Union*, Chabon uses alternative history to imagine that the United States established a provisional homeland for Jews that saved millions from the gas chambers and preserved Yiddish language and culture. This fiction is an oblique commentary on the historical reality that strict immigration quotas in the United States consigned many European Jews to death.

In the alternative present of *The Yiddish Policemen's Union*, Chabon's novelistic provisional homeland is about to "revert" sixty years after its founding, thus dispersing Sitka Jews once more. Hence, the status of Israel as a permanent Jewish state as well as the experience of

Jews in the diaspora is raised. Chabon imagines a world in which Israel does not yet exist and in which some ultra-Orthodox Jews, in league with an evangelical Christian U.S. government, are willing to use extreme and violent measures to rebuild the Temple. Thus, religious fundamentalism and violent masculinity become allied. However, this world without Israel is also one in which Jews are extremely vulnerable and are only allowed to be at home temporarily and on sufferance from the majority. Like Sitka, the Jewish kingdom of Khazaria in *Gentlemen of The Road* enables Jewish self-determination and diasporic wandering to be discussed in relation to one another rather than in opposition.

The Holocaust and Israel are often considered two pillars of Jewish identity, and Chabon certainly builds on these. Just as importantly, however, his work represents the differences between and among Jews and reflects that Jews are a diverse people. In *The Amazing Adventures of Kavalier and Clay*, Joe, as a refugee, has a different relationship to Nazism and the impending Holocaust than his American-born cousin, Sammy. In *The Yiddish Policemen's Union*, Chabon highlights the differences between secular Jews such as Landsman and traditionally observant Jews such as the Shpilman family. Often, hostility and tension exist between Orthodox and non-Orthodox Jews; thus, it is noteworthy that Landsman's partner and closest male friend, Berko Shemets, has chosen to live a commandment-driven life, including the observance of the Sabbath and the wearing of ritual garments. Chabon also refers to the tensions between different groups of observant Jews, also known as "black hats," in *The Yiddish Policemen's Union*. As Chabon's fiction has become more explicitly Jewish-centered, he has given the lie to any notion that there is one way to be Jewish. Indeed, his work seems to underscore the Jewish joke of "two Jews, three opinions." Taken together, his fictional worlds expand the purview of the contemporary Jewish writer as they entertain diverse ideas about masculinity, Jewishness, and Jewish masculinity.

DISCUSSION QUESTIONS

- Taking Chabon's fiction as a guide, what does it mean to be Jewish in the contemporary period?
- How does Chabon depict gay life, historically and in the contemporary period?
- What insights does Chabon's fiction provide on the challenges of marriage and the effects of divorce?

8

POP CULTURE IN MICHAEL CHABON'S WORK

Michael Chabon embraces rather than disdains popular culture. In his essay "Trickster in a Suit of Lights," he heralds entertainment as a value for writers and readers alike, and he refuses to accept that entertainment "means junk." Rather, he posits entertainment as a vehicle of human "exchange" and "connection," and thinks that escape and escapism have gotten an undeservedly bad reputation (*Maps and Legends,* 13, 17). In "The Killer Hook," Chabon discusses comics artist Howard Chaykin as an exemplar of a "pop artisan" who is "haunted by a vision of pop perfection: heartbreaking beauty that moves units" (*Maps and Legends,* 99). Chabon's own career demonstrates the porousness of the boundary between the artistic and the popular as his major novels have been adapted for the big screen, as he has increasingly worked within and against the conventions of genre fiction, and as his fictionalized history of the Golden Age of comics escaped the pages of his Pulitzer Prize–winning novel *The Amazing Adventures of Kavalier and Clay* and turned into a Dark Horse Comics series *The Amazing Adventures of the Escapist.*

AT THE MOVIES AND ON TV

Chabon belongs to the Writers Guild of America but has had limited success bringing his scripts to fruition. His TNT pilot project *Telegraph*

Avenue that features two California families—one black, one white—seems to have reached a dead end. Although he was called upon to work up an "early draft" for the *X-Men* movie, his ideas ended up in the reject pile. Chabon readily admits that his script *The Gentleman Host*, about older men who entertain women on cruises in exchange for free travel, represents his affinity for men of his grandfather's generation but isn't a particularly marketable idea. Chabon traveled to Beijing and Hong Kong for his work on a screenplay for Disney's *Snow and the Seven*, a martial-arts version of Snow White and the Seven Dwarfs set in late nineteenth century British-controlled Hong Kong; however, he was replaced as screenwriter so that the film could be taken in a "more fun" direction. For *Spiderman 2*, Chabon served as an "intermediate screenwriter"; that is, he worked on a screenplay already in progress and then turned it over to another writer.

The most frustrating screenwriting job that Chabon has undertaken is the script for the film adaptation of his novel *The Amazing Adventures of Kavalier and Clay*. Scott Rudin, a producer with a penchant for literary adaptations (including *Revolutionary Road* and *No Country for Old Men*), bought the rights to *Kavalier and Clay* and commissioned Chabon to write the script. By all reports, Rudin required multiple drafts and was more committed to the script closely adhering to the novel than the author himself. Chabon told *Entertainment Weekly* that his first draft was "from memory, as if there were no novel at all and I were just remembering a story that I had heard" ("IT Script"). Chabon felt that "a lot of things about the book are really a pain in the neck" to adapt for film, so he chose to focus the screenplay on the war period ("IT Script"). Speaking on the *Washington Post's Book World Live*, Chabon shared his perspective that "the book is the book, and the movie—if there ever is one—is the movie. They don't really have all that much to do with each other. They're like those twins who get separated as infants and raised on separate continents." For the film, Chabon added the actual marriage ceremony of Rosa and Sammy, a scene absent from the novel. Although Chabon completed the script, the film has remained in preproduction for years. The late Sydney Pollack was originally scheduled to direct the film; now Stephen Daldrey hopes to direct it. A promising cast was reportedly assembled: Tobey McGuire as Joe Kavalier and Natalie Portman as Rosa. However, in early 2009, Chabon reported that the project was in limbo due to financing issues.

Despite the frustrations of bringing *Kavalier and Clay* to the big screen, Chabon continues to have faith in Scott Rudin and his ability to eventually make the film. Such faith in Rudin is derived from the latter's role in not only making but also reissuing the critically successful adaptation of Chabon's second novel, *Wonder Boys*. Directed by Curtis Hanson (who also directed *L.A. Confidential*) and coproduced by Rudin and Hanson, the movie has an all-star cast, with Michael Douglas as Grady Tripp; Frances McDormand as Sara Gaskell, college chancellor and Tripp's married, pregnant lover; Robert Downey Jr. as Crabtree, Tripp's editor; and Tobey McGuire as James Leer. The soundtrack includes Bob Dylan's Oscar-winning "Things Have Changed." Steve Kloves wrote the screenplay for the movie, since at the time Chabon was in the process of writing *The Amazing Adventures of Kavalier and Clay*. Emily, Tripp's Korean American Jewish wife, is absent from the film, as is the Passover seder at the center of the novel. Chabon agreed with these changes, though at least one otherwise glowing review suggests that "the loss of ethnicity rankles without being ruinous" (Travers). Kloves's major addition is the character of the pregnant waitress, who functions as a double for Gaskell and a catalyst for Tripp's redemptive choice to choose a future as a husband, father, and writer. Overall, Chabon approves of the film, admiring its craft as well as McDormand's acting in particular. He does, however, note that the film gives short shrift to the wonder boy narrative in favor of Douglas's midlife crisis and that Douglas is "not an anti-star the way his character is an anti-hero" (Sragow).

As Michael Sragow reports in *Salon*, the film version of *Wonder Boys* was originally released in February after Academy Award nominations, a period that Kloves identifies as the "graveyard of pre-spring." Moreover, the marketing was "horrendous," according to Kloves. The trailer used Douglas and the dead dog as hooks, thus creating an impression of slapstick and undercutting the film's narrative substance. Given the generally favorable critical reception—*Rolling Stone*'s Peter Travers deemed it "a comic dazzler of roguish wit and touching gravity that is driven by characters, not jokes"—a new marketing campaign was devised, and the film was re-released. Echoing James Leer's pronouncement in the movie that writing means something, Sragow comments that "Making *Wonder Boys* was, for Hanson and Kloves and the cast, an act of faith that movies can mean something."

In sharp contrast to Hanson's *Wonder Boys*, the film adaptation of *The Mysteries of Pittsburgh*, directed and written by Rawson Marshall Thurber, received mostly negative, even scathing, reviews. Thurber, who directed *Dodgeball*, took significant liberties with Chabon's narrative, most notably turning the sexual confusion of Art Bechstein (played by Jon Foster) into his competing desire for Cleveland (Peter Sarsgaard) and for Jane, Cleveland's girlfriend (played by Sienna Miller). This love triangle minimizes the role of Phlox (Mena Suvari), while the gay character of Arthur Lecomte has been excised from the film. *The Mysteries of Pittsburgh* premiered at the 2008 Sundance festival and reached wider distribution more than a year later. Although Chabon wrote on his Web site in 2006 that "Mr. T's script is top-notch," *Entertainment Weekly*'s Owen Gleiberman deemed the film a "stillborn rendering" of Chabon's novel, while the *New York Times* categorized it as a "clumsy and confused adaptation" (Scott). During the filming of *Mysteries*, Sienna Miller's unflattering comments about Pittsburgh, which she ultimately retracted, created some early bad local press for the film.

The hard-boiled detective genre of Chabon's *The Yiddish Policemen's Union* lends itself to film adaptation; indeed, Scott Rudin purchased the film rights prior to the writing of the novel. Ethan and Joel Coen—who have *Fargo*, *Barton Fink*, and *No Country for Old Men* among their credits—are scheduled to write and direct *The Yiddish Policemen's Union*. Chabon responded to this news with much enthusiasm, proclaiming the Coen brothers "among [his] favorite living moviemakers" ("Oh, Brothers!").

A guest appearance on the "Moe'N'A Lisa" episode of *The Simpsons* furthered Chabon's status as a pop icon. Chabon's father told Steven Barrie-Anthony of the *Los Angeles Times* that, although he expected his son to win a Pulitzer Prize and anticipates a National Book Award in the future, he never dreamed that his offspring would be featured on *The Simpsons*. Chabon lent his voice to his own character. In this episode, Lisa arranges Moe's Post-it notes into a poem she titles "Howling at a Concrete Moon" and sends it off for publication in *American Poetry Perspectives*. Appearing at the Wordloaf Literary Festival (a spoof on the Bread Loaf Writers' Conference held annually at Middlebury College in Vermont), Moe fears that his literary celebrity would be endangered by acknowledging Lisa's contributions, so he passes himself off as poetically self-sufficient.

Chabon's character appears on a panel titled "Writers on Writing," which turns into a face-off with Jonathan Franzen, author of *The Corrections*. Tom Wolfe, the chair of the panel, invites "fawning praise and obvious questions" from the audience. When Chabon is asked about his influences, he cites Franzen and is miffed when Franzen does not return the favor, especially since Chabon "blurbed" Franzen. The literary competition between Franzen and Chabon continues after Moe experiences a change of heart and identifies Lisa as his "mini-muse."

When an emotional Chabon suggests that "you couldn't make this stuff up," Franzen turns that response into a personal insult: "*You* couldn't." At that point, Chabon decides that Franzen's "nose needs some corrections," and the two fight, complete with the "pows" of comic book conventions. Insider jokes abound. Chabon's relationship to comics is referenced and satirized by a shot of a picture of Snoopy on his doghouse (the famous funny paper dog penned by Charles Schulz had literary aspirations and was occasionally shown with a typewriter). The marquee at the entrance to the conference warns that "Philip Roth may be moody," thus reminding viewers of Chabon's links to Roth. At the end of the episode, the editor at the poetry journal demands photos of and poems about Spiderman, a sly allusion to Chabon's role as intermediate scriptwriter for *Spiderman 2* and also a reminder of the entanglements of the popular and the literary, a distinctive feature of Chabon's career.

A Serious Look at the Funny Papers

Michael Chabon's long love affair with comics exemplifies the use of popular culture in his works. One of Chabon's failed boyish adventures was the founding of the C.C.B.C, the Columbia (Maryland) Comic Book Club. A more successful adventure occurred on the way to a swimming pool, when he and a boyhood friend, towels draped around their shoulders like capes, assumed the superhero alter egos of Dark Lord and Aztec.

Years later, Chabon transformed this childhood memory into Joe Kavalier and Sammy Clay's cocreation of the Escapist, a superhero at the helm of the League of the Golden Key who, like Houdini, frees himself and others from literal and figurative iron chains. In his novel *The Amazing Adventures of Kavalier and Clay*, the comic book world takes center stage. For example, after Joe and Sammy come up with the initial idea for the Escapist, they decide to take a walk; the following chapter constitutes the origin story of the Escapist, and the chapter after that depicts the cocreators and their ad hoc creative team working up a sample issue of Radio Comics.

Later in the novel, when Sheldon Anapol, owner of Empire Comics, has reservations about a cover that features the Escapist punching Hitler in the jaw, Joe and Sammy threaten to take their popular character to another publisher. That chapter ends with the literary analogue of a comics cliffhanger: trying to determine whether their decision to leave with the Escapist is an idle threat or not, Sammy and Joe wait for an elevator. Toward the end of the novel, Joe Kavalier dons the costume of his creation and, using a safety belt of rubber bands, leaps from the Empire State Building and falls to a ledge a few stories below. Both narrative event and structure of *The Amazing Adventures of Kavalier and Clay* owe a debt to the reissued Golden Age comics that Chabon consumed as a child. Notably, as Chabon was plotting his next project after

Wonder Boys, he discovered in his attic the lone box of those comics which he had saved.

Embedded in *The Amazing Adventures of Kavalier and Clay* is the history of comics in the United States, from the advent of Shuster and Siegel's Superman, which ushered in the Golden Age of Comics, to the challenges the comic book industry faced from moral purity campaigns in the 1950s. At some points, mock footnotes contribute to the documentary texture of the novel. Equally important are the ways in which comic book history shapes the fictional adventures of Kavalier and Clay. Like the historical Joe Shuster and Jerome Siegel, Joe Kavalier and Sammy Clay do not receive their fair share of the profits from their creation, though Chabon has made clear that the historical progenitors of superheroes endured impoverishment that he did not visit upon his fictional characters. Similarly, Chabon fictionally revisits the chilling effect that real-life diatribes against comic books and their corrupting influence on the young had upon the comic book industry. Historically, the writings of psychiatrist Fredric Wertham, culminating in *The Seduction of the Innocent* (1954), encouraged the U.S. Senate Subcommittee to Investigate Juvenile Delinquency to focus its attention and to conduct hearings on comic books. In Chabon's novelistic universe, the fictional Sammy Clay testifies and is outed at these hearings.

Chabon's novel represents comics as an art form open to immigrants and ethnics not welcome in or educated for other, more prestigious commercial art fields. In particular, Chabon exposes the ways in which Jewishness became encoded in the development of the form. Joe's first attempt at drawing a superhero results in a portrait of the golem, a figure from Jewish legend who defends Jews from onslaughts of anti-Semitic violence but also tends to evade the control of his rabbinic creators and sometimes becomes a destructive force. Thus, the golem and the development of the superhero become linked as Jewish fantasies of self-defense, especially as superheroes are mobilized in the late 1930s and early 1940s to fight fascism. Moreover, for Jewish creators and readers alike, the superhero becomes an embodiment of masculine power in a culture that tends to view Jewish men stereotypically as bookish and feminized. When Joe first drew the golem in 1939, Sammy was appalled by the overt Jewishness of Joe's conception of the superhero. Yet by the end of the novel, set in 1954, Sammy emphasizes the Jewishness of superheroes: "Superman, you don't think he's Jewish. Coming over from the old country, changing his name like that. Clark Kent, only a Jew would pick a name like that for himself" (*Kavalier and Clay*, 585). Chabon's novel, in league with Art Spiegelman's graphic Holocaust novel *Maus*, has spawned journalistic and academic attention to the overlap between comic book history and Jewish history.

In a review of *The Amazing Adventures of Kavalier and Clay*, Ken Kalfus comments that the book "would make a nice comic book series." Beginning in 2004, Dark Horse Comics began the series *The Amazing Adventures of the Escapist*. To date, eight issues in four volumes have appeared. What if the Escapist really were a part of comic book history rather than a novelistic invention? What if Kavalier and Clay were historical comic book artists rather than fictional characters? Such questions become the premise for the *Escapist* series. The first issue opens with an introduction by Michael Chabon, in which he provides a faux history of the efforts to recover "the great lost superhero of the Golden Age" and his own first "discovery" of the comic in which the Escapist is shown "escaping from his own head." Critics and general readers often spar about whether art imitates life or life imitates art. This introduction and the series itself exemplify the ways in which art imitates art, as Chabon refers to his novel and the characters that Kavalier and Clay created within those pages.

A more detailed faux history appears later in the first issue of *The Amazing Adventures of the Escapist* under the title "Escapism 101," a feature written by "Malachi B. Cohen," an anagram of Michael Chabon. Quotations from Chabon's novel abound in "Escapism 101," but the history extends well beyond 1954, the year in which the novel ends, and charts the transformations that the Escapist undergoes under diverse legal and publishing arrangements. According to this faux history, a racial transformation occurred in 1966, underwritten by a black beauty products company, in which "the streets of Empire City were prowled by a black Escapist whose unique, historically based twist on the theme of enslavement and liberation remains a personal favorite of the author's."

The first episode of the first issue of Volume 1 of *The Amazing Adventures of the Escapist* is titled "The Passing of the Key." Written by Chabon, the episode translates the Escapist's origin story into the comics medium. In keeping with the father–son thematic dominant in Chabon's oeuvre, Tom Mayflower identifies Max as "the only father I ever knew" and is instructed by Omar to "honor his legacy." As in the novel, a boy with a limp is transformed into a superhero who vows to liberate all those who "toil in chains." Subsequent episodes are written by Kevin McCarthy, Howard Chaykin, and Brian Vaughn, among others.

Chaykin, about whose comic book series *American Flagg!* Chabon writes admiringly in *Maps and Legends*, contributed "Are You Now or Have You Ever Been . . . ," a storyline about Senator McCraven, a McCarthyite on a witch hunt for communists whose moral hypocrisy is revealed in the red-light district. At the end of the episode, the Escapist is depicted as a lady's man. Here his absolute righteousness is put into question, a trend that continues in other episodes, most notably "Sequestered," in which the iron chain ring has infiltrated the judicial system even as the Escapist's rush to judgment is revealed. In comics writer Kevin McCarthy's "Prison Break," the Escapist provides a literary lesson on Frankenstein to a jailor associated with a plan to turn all of Empire City into a prison. To thwart this plot, the Escapist receives help from the bomb-savvy Saboteur, the Aryan-American League nemesis in Chabon's novel.

The Escapists, issues 7 and 8, shifts the focus to the creators of the Escapist and the attempts of Kavalier and Clay's heirs to uphold the legacy of those Golden Age comic book wonder boys. Volume 3 of the series won an Eisner Award for best anthology and a Harvey Award for best new comics series. Although in a review of Volume 1, Gordon Flagg categorizes the Dark Horse series as "above-average mainstream superhero exploits that probably appeal more to comics aficionados than readers of the novel," those familiar with *The Amazing Adventures of Kavalier and Clay* should recognize that many of the storylines and themes derive from Chabon's novelistic details.

A Pulitzer Prize–Winning Genre Writer

The Amazing Adventures of Kavalier and Clay has been called an "ode to mass culture" (Caldwell, "An Ode to the Golden Age") and a "love song" to the comic book (Lotozo). Prior to *Kavalier and Clay*, Chabon had intimated his interests in popular culture and genre fiction; as he points out, gangsters do figure prominently in *The Mysteries of Pittsburgh*. In *Wonder Boys*, horror fiction is given its due in the portrait of Albert Vetch, aka August Van Zorn, the first writer that Grady Tripp ever met. Van Zorn indirectly facilitates Grady's friendship with Crabtree: the two meet in a creative writing class in which Tripp has paraphrased and Crabtree has plagiarized outright one of Van Zorn's stories. Notably, Chabon pens the final story of his collection *Werewolves in Their Youth* under Zorn's fictional name. Thus, early in his career, Chabon imagines a genre writer as an authorial alter ego for both himself and his writer characters.

According to Chabon, writing *Kavalier and Clay* clarified his love for popular culture and genre fiction, and the success of the novel overcame the shame that he had come to associate with this love. Talking with Gregory Kirschling of *Entertainment Weekly*, he posits that this was a "process analogous to coming out." On many occasions, he has indicated that his ideal bookstore would contain one "fiction" section rather than a section for "literature" separated from those dedicated to genres such as mystery and adventure. For Chabon, popular genres and aesthetic quality can and do coexist. Indeed, in *Kavalier and Clay*, Chabon, through the character of Joe Kavalier, makes an argument for comics as a serious art form and defends escapism as an aesthetic value. Joe's championing of pop art reflects the course of Chabon's own career.

The Yiddish Policemen's Union is a love song to the hard-boiled detective novel, and Chabon reports that he was under the influence of Raymond Chandler, Dashiell Hammett, and Ross McDonald while writing it. Before this "big" novel, however, Chabon took the plunge into detective fiction with the shorter work of *The Final Solution: A Story of Detection*. The English detective of *The Final Solution* is an old man who remains unnamed throughout the novella. However, the initial description of him as one who "had once made his fortune and his reputation through a long and brilliant series of extrapolations from unlikely groupings of facts" (2) as well as the detailed descriptions of his beekeeping suggests that he is none other than an aged, retired Sherlock Holmes. For the Holmes fan, such as Chabon, the title of the work not only refers to Holocaust history but also to the Sir Arthur Conan Doyle story "The Adventure of the Final Problem" in which Holmes supposedly dies. Chabon's title also alludes to Nicholas Meyer's novel *The Seven-Per-Cent Solution,* which speculates on Holmes's activities after he disappears in "The Final Problem" and prior to his return in "The Adventure of the Empty House."

The Final Solution's Linus Steinman, a Jewish boy of nine, has escaped from Nazi Germany and resides at a boarding house run by a black Anglican vicar, Mr. Panicker, and his wife. Linus's closest companion is his parrot, Bruno, who has many readers speculating about the significance of the numerical sequence that he ritualistically chants in German. When a new lodger, Mr. Shane, turns up dead and Bruno goes missing, the unnamed Holmes, quite fragile with age, is ousted from retirement at the behest of an Inspector Bellowes and over the objections of Detective Constable Quint. Although the Panickers' son, Reggie, is the prime suspect, Holmes establishes that he is only guilty of stealing the contents of another lodger's wallet. Mr. Parkins, the victim of Reggie's theft, is a government operative as was Mr. Shane; believing the numbers that Bruno recites might be important German code, the government fears that a German spy has murdered Shane and taken Bruno. In a section of the novella narrated from the perspective of the parrot, imprisoned in a laundry sack in a closet, we learn that Mr. Kalb, a member of the Aid Committee that rescued Linus, is the killer of Shane and the kidnapper of Bruno. Kalb's motive was greed: he believed that the parroted German numerical sequence represented Swiss bank account numbers. Together, Mr. Panicker, a vicar who has lost his religious faith, and Holmes, a detective who avers that the meaning of Bruno's numbers will remain one of "the insoluble problems . . . that reflected the true nature of things" (*Solution*, 131), reunite Bruno with Linus. In that reunion, Bruno sings the "train song" to Linus in mimicry of the latter's mother, "whom none of them would ever meet or see again" (*Solution*, 131). Thus, Chabon uses the conventions of the detective story to offer, as he did in *The Amazing Adventures of Kavalier and Clay*, a meditation on loss. In *The Final Solution*, as in *Kavalier and Clay*, art, or an artful voice, can memorialize but not compensate for the losses associated with the twentieth century, even and especially those of the Holocaust.

In *Gentlemen of the Road*, Chabon turns to the genre of adventure and shifts his Jewish historical interests from the twentieth century to the more distant past. This tale, whose working title was "Jews with Swords," is Michael Chabon's attempt as a writer to emulate his characters and go "off in search of a little adventure" (*Gentlemen of the Road*, "Afterword"). He does so by setting this episodic tale, which originally appeared in installments in the *New York Times Magazine*, in Khazaria, a medieval Jewish kingdom situated between the Black and Caspian Seas. (A map of the world that Chabon's gentlemen wander is usefully included in the inside back cover of the novella.) The Jewish gangsters of *The Mysteries of Pittsburgh* have been transformed into the swashbuckling buddies Zelikman, a Frankish Jew, and Amram, an Abyssinian Jew. Chabon treats this odd couple with irony but also affection. Although they verbally abuse one another with alarming regularity, such gruff habits of being are symptomatic of the friendship that substitutes for family they have lost and "the solitude that they had somehow contrived to share" (*Gentlemen*, 196). The melancholy Zelikman, attached to his horse named Hillel and his hat, has wandered from his Regensburg home. Estranged from his father, he mourns his mother and his sister, victims of anti-Semitic mob violence. Amram, who trusts in his ax, "the Mother-Defiler," began his wanderings in search of his kidnapped daughter and remained on the road. Zelikman, like his creator, is intrigued by the notion of a place "where a Jew rules over other Jews as king" (*Gentlemen*, 22). Thus, he, Amram, and a Muslim army fight battle after battle in their mercenary quest to help Filaq, a young stripling Khazar prince, return to and reclaim a usurped kingdom. As in Chabon's other fictions, escapistry and transvestism enliven the pages, as do the thematics of male friendship and Jewish identity defined by exile. For Chabon, thematic substance and genre fiction are compatible; indeed, he categorizes *Gentlemen of the Road* as a work with "serious thematic concerns" that hopefully "wears them rather lightly" (Siegel).

Chabon's works have become increasingly Jewish-centered at the same time that he has been returning to and refurbishing the "ghetto" of genre. Aesthetically and culturally, he has resisted assimilation and has constructed a creative and popular home for himself not only on book-shelves but also on the big screen.

DISCUSSION QUESTIONS

- How are Jewishness and popular cultural forms interwoven in Chabon's novels?
- Do you consider the film adaptations of Chabon's novels to be better, worse, equal to, or merely different from the books? Why? What transformations have taken place as these stories have moved from page to screen?
- Has your knowledge of and opinion of comic books changed as a result of reading *The Amazing Adventures of Kavalier and Clay*? How?

9

MICHAEL CHABON ON THE INTERNET

From early on in his career, Michael Chabon has used the Internet to communicate with his readers, and his fans have used virtual reality to communicate with one another about his writing, his public appearances, and film adaptations of his novels. His critics, too, have made ample use of technology. For those who want to see Chabon and hear him read his work—and answer questions about it—YouTube can be a useful site to explore. Given the fluidity of Internet content, the reader should not despair if something discussed here becomes unavailable; other e-sources are sure to appear.

When Michael Chabon first published *Wonder Boys*, he included his e-mail on the book, making him one of the first writers to initiate such communication between author and audience. In the first months after publication, Chabon received hundreds of messages, almost all of them attesting to the pleasures and life transformations that his writing had brought to his readers. Such messages provided Chabon with reciprocal pleasure; as he put it, "All I knew before was what critics thought. To have these concrete, personal, emotional responses is such a—forgive the pun—novel experience" (Streitfeld, "Cyberstrokes"). However, keeping up with e-mail correspondence at the level that he thought his readers deserved became too time-consuming; to keep in touch with his dedicated audience, he developed a Web site that was quite well-maintained from 1999 until his sign-off in November 2006. It contained links to essays previously published elsewhere, such as his introduction to *McSweeney's Enchanted Chamber of Astonishing Stories*, as well as a link to "Hollywoodland" in which he posted "An Account of a Brief Bout of Mutant Madness," a chronicle of his rejected treatment for the *X-Men* movie. However, this virtual project proved too difficult and time-consuming to keep updated, and he was unwilling to turn over the maintenance of the Web site to someone else. Thus, with regret, Chabon discontinued his extensive virtual communiqués with readers. An archived version of this Web site can be found at Wayback Machine, a Web archive (see http://web.archive.org/web/*/michaelchabon.com).

Chabon's current official Web site, www.michaelchabon.com, is a simple affair, its main feature being a calendar listing some of his public appearances. Its home page is occasionally updated with current happenings or writings; for example, during the 2008 election season, it featured links to his essays related to the Obama campaign; in 2009 it announced his work on the screenplay for the Disney film *John Carter of Mars*, based on the writing of Edgar Rice Burroughs, and the publication of his essay collection *Manhood for Amateurs*. For Chabon, time spent on the Internet represents competition for precious writing time. He confesses that he is a bit of an Internet junkie and has joked about his need for Internet Anonymous. However, he also makes good use of the Internet as a research tool, and in a *New York Times* feature in which he answered readers' questions, he listed several Internet sources that he used for his depiction of the Jewish kingdom of Khazaria featured in *Gentlemen of the Road*.

Although Chabon has limited the time that he spends with his readers on the Internet of late, his very successful writer-wife, Ayelet Waldman, maintains an active virtual life. Her blog *Living Out Loud Online* used to be hosted at Salon.com; now she posts regularly at www.ayeletwaldman.com. Some of these entries provide details about her domestic life with Chabon and their four children; she also chronicles events at which she and Chabon appear together. Notably, she blogged about their joint appearance at the White House "Evening of Poetry, Music and the Spoken Word" in May 2009. Waldman, a lawyer and a former district attorney, was a classmate of Barack Obama at Harvard Law School; both she and Chabon campaigned strenuously for him during the 2008 presidential campaign. On her blog, she reported that she and Chabon were invited to the White House by "dint of much confusion regarding the extent of our cool." In their "White House Shtick" ("shtick" is Yiddish for routine or performance), they riffed on the need to use one's words to get to know and empathize with the stranger. Given Waldman's use of the Internet, Chabon's virtual presence is a family affair.

When Chabon signed off of his Web site in November 2006, he encouraged readers to consult *The Amazing Website of Kavalier and*

Clay (see http://www.sugarbombs.com/kavalier/), which offers "the freshest information at a low, low price." Nate Raymond, owner of *The Amazing Website*, uses Chabon's quotation as the tagline for his fan site. Included on this extensive site are descriptions of and links to articles, reviews, and interviews related to Michael Chabon, as well as information about Chabon's fiction, film adaptations of his novels, screenwriting projects, the Escapist comics, Ayelet Waldman, awards, and lectures/readings. One notable link is to the covers of Chabon's books, including international editions.

McSweeney's is a literary journal, edited by novelist Dave Eggers, as well as a modest publishing house. Chabon has had a long association with McSweeney's as both a contributor and editor. McSweeney's Internet site hosts an author page devoted to Michael Chabon (http://mcsweeneys.net/authorpages/chabon/chabon.html) that includes links to biographical information, a list of his works, films, and awards, as well as press and interviews. As the publisher of Chabon's *Maps and Legends*, McSweeney's also features a page devoted to this work (http://mcsweeneys.net/books/mapsandlegends/). The page includes both a description of this collection of essays and links to published reviews of it. To celebrate the publication of *Maps and Legends*, McSweeney's posted a link to Chabon's *Spiderman 2* script for a short period in 2008; a very brief excerpt from that script remains on the site (http://mcsweeneys.net/2008/4/11chabon.html).

Literary bloggers tend to keep up with Michael Chabon and his work. The Millions (www.themillions.com), known for its arts and culture coverage, has excerpts from Chabon's expansive but now defunct Web site as well as more recent news and commentary about his career. As a winner of the science fiction Hugo Award for *The Yiddish Policemen's Union*, Chabon is oft-mentioned on io9 (http://io9.com), a science fiction blog site initiated in 2008 by Gawker Media. Charlie Jane Anders, an associate editor at io9, wrote a piece focused on Chabon's vision of Dr. Octopus in his script for *Spiderman 2* and the superiority of that depiction compared to the final script. Anders's opinion elicited a great deal of commentary from io9 readers. Also on the io9 site is Austin Grossman's report of Michael Chabon's appearance at the 2009 Wondercon, an annual convention devoted to comic books, science fiction, and related films.

Because Chabon is an active screenwriter as well as a novelist whose works have been adapted for film or are in preproduction, The Internet Movie Database (www.imdb.com) includes a profile of him. The site features links to both *Wonder Boys* (2000) and *The Mysteries of Pittsburgh* (2008), as well as trailers for both films. The announcement that Chabon had been hired to revise Andrew Stanton and Mark Andrews's script for Disney's *John Carter of Mars* dominated the Chabon-related news on IMDb in Spring 2009.

Chabon has a strong virtual presence on several Jewish-related sites. He participated in the podcast series *Voices on Antisemitism* (www. ushmm.org/museum/exhibit/focus/antisemitism/voices/transcript/?content= 20080313), sponsored by the United States Holocaust Memorial Museum. In that interview, Chabon discusses his grappling with the ethics of Holocaust representation in his work, in particular the destruction of Yiddish and Yiddish-speakers that was the focus of his essay on Beatrice and Uriel Weinrich's *Say It in Yiddish: A Phrase Book for Travelers* and that he tried to imaginatively counteract in *The Yiddish Policemen's Union*. Controversy about that essay, "Guidebook to a Land of Ghosts," first circulated on the academic Yiddish listserv Mendele (http://mendele. commons.yale.edu) in June and July 1997. Though a few of these entries are in Yiddish, most are in English. Included in the Mendele archives is Chabon's June 29, 1997, response to the controversy, in which he avows, "I love Yiddish. I love being Jewish. I love language and humor. . . . The desire to hurt, offend, or insult Yiddish scholars and lovers of Yiddish did not make up even one atom of my motivation." One commentator suggested that "Mr. Chabon needs to learn more about both Yiddish history and language usage"; Chabon took such advice to heart in his research for and writing of *The Yiddish Policemen's Union*. JBooks (http://jbooks. com), which identifies itself as "the online Jewish book community," has several features on Chabon, including a piece titled "Holy Yiddishkeit, Batman!" by Jewish studies scholar Jeffrey Shandler and an interview with Chabon titled "The Language Deep, Deep in Chabon's Ear," conducted by Todd Hasak-Lowy.

Diverse Chabon-related videos are available on YouTube. Michael Chabon reads from *Gentlemen of the Road* for the first time in "Story Hour in the Library," professionally recorded at the University of California–Berkeley in September 2008. In the question and answer session, Chabon discusses writing the screenplay for *Kavalier and Clay* and wittily reports that, during this long process, he "came to despise the author of the novel." He also compares his composing process for *The Yiddish Policemen's Union* with that for *Gentlemen of the Road*.

In a December 2007 interview on the Jewish Television Network (http://www.youtube.com/watch?v=Ldq10VQD3Io), Chabon talks with Brad Greenberg about his relationship to Israel and his desire to imagine daily life in Yiddish for both religious and secular Jews in *The Yiddish Policemen's Union*. In a video shot at a Barnes and Noble bookstore in San Jose, California, Chabon reads from *The Yiddish Policemen's Union* (http://www.youtube.com/watch?v=HuA__E5CIkg); in the question and answer session (http://www.youtube.com/watch?v=U0zyYr8Kf60), he traces his interest in alternative history to a *National Lampoon* magazine special issue devoted to the premise that Jackie Kennedy rather than JFK was assassinated in 1963. Fourth Estate, Chabon's British publisher, used the conventions of noir to advertise *The Yiddish Policemen's Union* on television; that ad can be seen on YouTube. Chabon's appearance with Ayelet Waldman at the White House has been posted on that popular video site, as has Chabon's endorsement of Barack Obama.

Several short production diary entries for the film *The Mysteries of Pittsburgh* are available on YouTube; one of these includes a shot of Michael Chabon on the set. YouTube is also a place where fans have paid homage to his work. A notable example is a Czech fan film adaptation of *The Amazing Adventures of Kavalier and Clay* by Petr and Havel Hruby. The ten-minute sequence focuses on the meeting between Sammy and Joe and the creation of the Escapist, and also features flashbacks to Joe saying goodbye to his brother in Prague as well as a headline that announces Thomas's ultimate fate: "U-boat Sinks Mercy Ship."

Ultimately, Chabon's virtual presence on the Internet is a case study for the ways in which technology continues to transform and expand our understanding of contemporary authors, their works, and their readers' experiences.

DISCUSSION QUESTIONS

- How and why has Chabon's use of the Internet changed during the course of his career? How might readers make use of his Web site?
- Are fan sites ever academically useful? How can you assess the reliability of information found on such sites?
- Which Chabon-related sites are up-to-date? Which contain outdated information?

10

MICHAEL CHABON AND THE MEDIA

As a Pulitzer Prize–winning author, Michael Chabon and his books receive a great deal of media attention which reflects and shapes literary reputations. A new book by Chabon is almost always reviewed by the *New York Times*, the *Washington Post*, the *Los Angeles Times*, the *Boston Globe*, and *Salon* as well as by Canada's *Globe and Mail* and the United Kingdom's the *Guardian* and the *Times*. Interviews with him appear with some regularity in these publications and on National Public Radio (NPR). As Chabon's works have become increasingly and explicitly Jewish-centered, he has become a subject of great interest in the Jewish press. Given his penchant for genre fiction as well as his Hollywood presence as a screenwriter and as a novelist whose written work has been adapted into films, popular publications such as *Newsweek*, *Time*, and *Entertainment Weekly* often feature him and his work. His expertise in comic book history, represented by his novel *The Amazing Adventures of Kavalier and Clay* and the related comic book series *The Amazing Adventures of The Escapist*, has resulted in his appearance in comics-related documentaries.

THE REVIEWERS WEIGH IN

Much of the press on Chabon's first novel, *The Mysteries of Pittsburgh*, centered on his extreme youth, the fact that a professor sent the manuscript to his own agent without Chabon's knowledge, and the publishers' bidding war that resulted in one of the highest advances paid at that time for a first novel. F. Scott Fitzgerald's influence was oft-noted; in a *Globe and Mail* review, Marc Cote categorized the character of Cleveland as a "cross between Jay Gatsby and James Dean." Writing for the *New York Times Book Review* in a piece titled "Gangsters and Pranksters," Alice McDermott, an award-winning writer herself, declared Chabon a writer of promise, "clearly in love with language" and committed to plot in ways unusual for contemporary novelists. Highlighting these qualities of Chabon's writing has become a critical trend as his career has evolved. McDermott did chide Chabon for a lack of "well-developed characters." Noting Art's absent mother and the "emotionally flat" Phlox, McDermott's review anticipated an ongoing discussion about Chabon's portrayal of female characters. Erroneously conflating subject matter and the voice of the novel's narrator with the writer himself, *Newsweek* included Chabon on a list of contemporary gay writers.

With the publication of *Wonder Boys*, reviewers canonized Chabon as a major American novelist. Michiko Kakutani, a notoriously discerning reviewer for the *New York Times*, characterized Chabon's writing as that of "a magical spider, effortlessly spinning out elaborate webs of words that ensnare the reader with their beauty and style." Like Michael Gorra of the *New Republic*, Kakutani compared Chabon to Philip Roth. However, Kakutani experienced a disjunction between the serious and comic parts of *Wonder Boys*, declaring it to have a "split personality." Given that Chabon did not realize that parts of the novel were funny until he witnessed Ayelet Waldman's response to the novel, it is notable that some reviewers focused on the comic dimensions of the work; Bharat Tandon, writing for the (U.K.) *Times Literary Supplement*, characterized *Wonder Boys* as a "cynical comedy of literary fame," while Richard Eder declared it a "comic odyssey" in the *Los Angeles Times Book Review*. With a light-hearted allusion to *Don Quixote*, Eder treats the narrator of the novel with irony as he comments that "Grady's picaresque adventures would be travels, not with but of a donkey." The extended description in *Wonder Boys* of a seder at the family home of Tripp's Korean-born Jewish wife drew the attention of some reviewers in the Jewish press. Writing for Philadelphia's *Jewish Exponent*, Sanford Pinsker sees Chabon following in Philip Roth's footsteps as a satirist of Jewish life; he reads the Passover scene as "yet another chapter in the comic history of how Jewish-American writers conduct a seder."

Jonathan Yardley's review of *Wonder Boys* for the *Washington Post Book World* has remained one of the most influential, glowing, and most-quoted commentaries on Chabon. In this review, Yardley declares Chabon to be "stupendously gifted and accomplished"; he defines him as "the young star of American letters" who represents "brightly shining hope" rather than "cheap celebrity." With this latter comment, Yardley seeks to distinguish Chabon from the so-called brat pack novelists Bret Easton Ellis and Jay McInerney with whom he had been compared after the publication of *The Mysteries of Pittsburgh*. In his commentary, Yardley attends to the theme of male friendship, which has become a dominant issue in Chabon's work and oft-noted by reviewers. Although Yardley ends his review with the complimentary "wonder boys, wonder book," he does note the limits of first-person narration that Chabon uses in both *The Mysteries of Pittsburgh* and *Wonder Boys* and challenges him to "explore larger worlds" in future work. Chabon has commented that Yardley's avuncular advice echoed his own ambitions for the next stage of his career.

In *The Amazing Adventures of Kavalier and Clay*, Chabon succeeds in producing a novel with a significantly expanded scope, a quality noted by many reviewers. Janet Maslin of the *New York Times* emphasizes its bigness: "big settings (the top of the Empire State Building), big creative leaps (*Citizen Kane* plays a role here) and big historical relevance." Amy Benfer reads the novel's historical sweep as "a version of the 20th century both thrillingly recognizable and all his own." Gail Caldwell, writing for the *Boston Globe*, finds "its reach and dynamism" a harbinger of a promising future for the novel as a literary form; ultimately, she pronounces *Kavalier and Clay* a "novel that actually matters" ("An Ode to the Golden Age").

The status of comic books as an art form elicits a good bit of critical discussion. In a second review in the *New York Times* (works deemed significant often have two reviews devoted to them, one in a weekday edition of the paper and the other in the Sunday *Book Review*), Ken Kalfus notes that Chabon makes an argument for the "craftsmanship, provocative themes, and the artist's personal investment" in comics. In the *Independent*, Graham Caveney reads *Kavalier and Clay* as intertwining the comic book with the great American novel; similarly, Michael Dirda, writing for the *Washington Post*, views the novel, in part, as a meditation about the relationship between the comic book and the American dream.

Resistant to the blurred boundaries between high art and popular forms, David Horspool of the (U.K.) *Times Literary Supplement* notes that while the novel represents Chabon's "general interest in the trashier, pulpy end of American letters," Chabon's literary prose is distinctive from this trash. In one of the few dismissals of this novel, Steve Jelbert, a reviewer for the (U.K.) *Times* suggested that "this convoluted tribute to a famously concise form is unlikely to impress many ordinary people." The fact that the novel received positive coverage in *Entertainment Weekly* and *Newsweek* belies this critical assessment. In the pages of *O, the Oprah Magazine*, Nora Ephron identifies *The Amazing Adventures of Kavalier and Clay* as a novel inducing such rapture that she found herself still residing in its fictional world a week after finishing it.

Overall, *The Amazing Adventures of Kavalier and Clay* was glowingly received, and its winning a Pulitzer Prize as well as nominations for both the PEN/Faulkner Award and the National Book Award attests to its critical acclaim. However, a few reviewers found themselves distanced from characters and events. Jonathan Levi, writing for the *Los Angeles Times Book Review* read the book dispassionately and, in the pages of *Commentary*, John Podhoretz expressed his lack of readerly identification with Joe, whom he experienced as an "impossibly grand character." In sharp contrast to Janet Maslin's emphasis on the bigness of the work, Podhoretz deemed it a "small" book. The *Advocate*'s reviewer, David Bahr, noted the novel's depictions of New York's gay life and highlighted the "unforgettably touching gay kiss atop the Empire State Building." Referencing the early tendency to misread Chabon as a gay writer, Bahr notes Chabon's appreciation of his gay readers. Several critics, including Gerald Jonas, who reviewed *Kavalier and Clay* for the *Forward*, mention the underdevelopment of Rosa's character and relate that quality to the boy-centeredness of comic books as a genre.

The role of the golem is frequently discussed in reviews: both Jonathan Levi and Sheli Teitelbaum, a reviewer for the *Jerusalem Report*, focus on the golem as a metaphor for creation, while Kalfus reads the golem in *Kavalier and Clay* as emblematic of Chabon's emphasis on "the incantatory power of the word." For Podhoretz, the golem functions as a symbol of the Shoah's victims. Allison Kaplan Sommer, a reviewer for *Moment* magazine, reads *Kavalier and Clay* as indicating a shift in Chabon's identifications as a writer; according to her assessment, his earlier work "had Jewish elements, but not Jewish themes."

Reviews of both *The Final Solution* and *Gentlemen of the Road* highlighted Chabon's investments in genre fiction and his insistence that such literature should not be written off as inferior. According to the *New York Times* reviewer Deborah Friedell, *The Final Solution* is evidence for Chabon's claim that detective fiction and literary quality are not oxymoronic. Novelist Melvin Bukiet, writing for the *Washington Post*, objects to the use of the Holocaust as the backdrop for a mystery, while Josh Lambert of the *Forward* lauds Chabon for creating "an immensely resonant and original figure of the survivor." Lev Grossman, writing for *Time*, reads the erosion of the boundary between literary and popular fiction as the future, which "looks like it's going to be a page-turner" ("Pop Goes the Literature"). Grossman also reviewed *Gentlemen of the Road* for *Time* and read that short novel as a continuation of Chabon's "hot, star-crossed flirtation with the 'popular' genres" ("The Genius Who Wanted to Be a Hack"). Steve Almond of the *Boston Globe* reads Amram and Zelikman as "deeply in love," while Dennis Moore in *USA Today* regards them as very different Jewish types than those previously found in Chabon's work. *Guardian* reviewer Christopher Tayler suggests that while Chabon indulges in a "romantic dream of Jewish history," he falls into Jewish stereotyping in *Gentlemen of the Road*.

However, Tayler's critique of Chabon's depiction of Jews was mild compared to some responses to *The Yiddish Policemen's Union*. The sensationalistic *New York Post* portrayed the book as rabidly anti-Zionist and anti-Semitic. Citing the "novelist's ugly view of Jews," The *Post* suggested that Mel Gibson might be the appropriate director for the film adaptation of the book. The *Boston Globe*'s Gail Caldwell, who had previously written glowingly about *Kavalier and Clay*, found this novel "borderline offensive" ("The Long Shalom"). Yiddish scholar Ruth Wisse declared in the pages of *Commentary* that this Jewish hard-boiled detective novel represents an "in-group mugging." She views Chabon as fictionally dissolving the state of Israel, as knowing little about Yiddish and the European Jews who spoke it, and as writing for those who are similarly ignorant. Labeling him a "babe in Yiddishland," Wisse ultimately deems him as writing without a conscience and reducing Yiddish to "shlock and shtick." In a review that appeared in both the *Jerusalem Post* and the *Jewish Exponent*, Samuel Freedman also reads the novel as anti-Israel, writing that "the Promised Land is for Chabon more like Original Sin" and that this work constitutes a "love letter to exile and dispossession." Writing for the *Nation*, William Deresiewicz sees the imaginary setting of *The Yiddish Policemen's Union* as a symptom that Chabon and other contemporary Jewish American writers must look elsewhere for Jewish meaning.

Yet, many other reviewers celebrated *The Yiddish Policemen's Union* as emblematic of the contemporary Jewish literary renaissance. According to Mark Oppenheimer of the *Forward*, "with this novel, Chabon has joined the community of Jewish Jewish writers at the moment of its renewed efflorescence." In response to the *New York Post*'s vitriolic critique of the novel, Oppenheimer told Gawker Media that *The Yiddish Policemen's Union* engages with Yiddish culture in ways which are beyond the capabilities of most writers of Chabon's generation. Similarly, Sanford Pinsker, who expressed skepticism about Chabon's depiction of the seder in *Wonder Boys*, celebrated the Yiddishized landscape of Sitka and lauds Chabon for the wonderful "character portrait" of Rabbi Heskel Shpilman (2007). Joshua Furst of *Zeek* understands Chabon's project in *The Yiddish Policemen's Union* as striving to "imagine Jewish community" anew, while Vince Passaro in *O, the Oprah Magazine* views the novel as a form of homage to the "half-remembered, half-imagined" community of European Yiddish speakers. On the question of whether the novel is post-Zionist and thus potentially anti-Israel, or Zionist and thus pro-Israel, *Jerusalem Post* reviewer Gil Troy posits that *The Yiddish Policemen's Union* shows the need of Jews for a home of their own. Ruth Franklin, writing for *Slate*, avers that reading this "tough-talking, scrappy and open-hearted" novel for a clear political message "is as impossible as it is misguided." Simultaneously affirming Chabon's Jewish and literary credentials in the pages of the *New York Times*, Terence Rafferty declares Chabon "a rabbi of the sect of Story."

Discussions of Meyer Landsman and his status as a hard-boiled detective figure abound in reviews of *The Yiddish Policemen's Union*. Michiko Kakutani deems Landman "one of the most appealing detective heroes to come along since Sam Spade or Philip Marlowe" (Spade is the creation of Dashiell Hammett; Marlowe of Raymond Chandler). Daniel Schifrin, writing for *New York Jewish Week*, dubs Landsman the "Jewish everyman," and both Brian Braiker of *Newsweek* and Connie Ogle of the *Miami Herald* suggest that the solving of his case becomes a means of redemption for the detective. Mark Oppenheimer ultimately finds the characters stronger than the plot, which he thinks ends in confusion. Deresiewicz also takes issues with the ending; he posits that the conventions of the hard-boiled detective novel are an inadequate vehicle for the geopolitical events that unfold. While Deresiewicz thinks that Chabon becomes trapped by the prescriptions associated with genre fiction, Franklin reads Chabon as a writer who "makes the genres expand to take him in."

THE ART OF INTERVIEWS

Michael Chabon is profoundly generous about granting interviews and forthcoming in them; thus, there are many published conversations with him in the print press. He frequently talks with commentators on NPR (National Public Radio), and transcripts of those interviews are available. Media interest in him increased dramatically after *The Amazing Adventures of Kavalier and Clay* won the Pulitzer Prize. That novel has been a catalyst for heightened interest in comic books and their history, and Chabon is often interviewed for features on and documentaries about superheroes and their creators. He has appeared on *CBS Sunday Morning*, and his embrace of genre fiction has resulted in attention from the popular press. Chabon's deepening engagement with Jewish themes has made him a frequent interviewee in the national and regional Jewish press. New publications as well as author appearances are often the catalyst for interviews.

In an NPR interview with Liane Hansen about *Wonder Boys*, Michael Chabon talks about his depictions of writers in that novel and his own sense of an "other self" in control when writing. Chabon, in conversation with Lisa See of *Publishers Weekly*, was honest about the pressure of advances as he related the saga of his failed attempts to turn *Fountain City* into a publishable work. With *Boston Globe's* Joseph Kahn, Chabon shared that his life as a baseball fan informed *Fountain City* and that he, like Grady Tripp, quit smoking pot because "it keeps you from getting things done." Chabon identifies "the absolute poverty of male friendships" as an American tragedy in his interview with Craig Wilson that appeared in *USA Today*; relatedly, he talks briefly about a gay relationship he had during college and the fact that both he and Ayelet, singly and together, have always had communities of gay friends.

Shortly after the publication of *The Amazing Adventures of Kavalier and Clay*, Chabon talked with NPR's Terry Gross. In that interview, Chabon provides his own family history of comic books, with his grandfather, a printer, making the latest issues a staple of his father's New York childhood; Chabon's father continued this practice with his own son. Since Golden Age comics were reissued during Chabon's boyhood, he read the same comics that his father had readily consumed as a youth. Thus, the adventures of superheroes functioned as a cross-generational link. This interview also includes a discussion of the changes in comic books during the post–World War II era and as a result of the hearings of the Senate Subcommittee to Investigate Juvenile Delinquency. Chabon covers similar ground in his interview with Scott Tobias, but with more specifics about the work of Jack Kirby and Will Eisner's conviction that comic books are a legitimate art form.

Talking with Mark Binelli and Bryce Duffy of *Rolling Stone* after winning the Pulitzer Prize, Chabon reminisces about his childhood collaboration with a friend to form Nova Comics, which featured the characters of Dark Lord and Aztec. Discussing his early success as a writer, he says it took him "a few years to catch up" with the reality of being a published author rather than a graduate student trying to finish his thesis. During the composition of *Kavalier and Clay*, he listened to big band music in order to evoke the period about which he was writing. He relies on a stable family life and a regular routine to do the work of novel writing, which is "about getting your work done and getting your work done every day."

In yet another interview with NPR and Terry Gross, this one related to the publication of *The Yiddish Policemen's Union*, Chabon notes that the *What If?* Marvel Comics series was his first exposure to a counter-factual narrative. The short-lived plan by Harold Ickes, Roosevelt's Secretary of the Interior, to use Alaska as a refuge for Jews fleeing Nazi-occupied Europe and Congressional delegate Anthony Dimond's successful campaign against this proposal provided the germ for his fictional mapping of Sitka, Alaska. In relation to his depiction of Sitka, he discusses the diversity of and divisions among Jews in Israel.

Talking with Stuart Jeffries of the *Guardian*, Chabon asserts that he was striving to achieve the intimacy of in-group identification with his use of "yid" in the novel. He also expresses his belief that Yiddish and the hard-boiled detective genre share a "sentimental and a cold-eyed view of what human beings can expect from the world." During a conversation with Patricia Cohen of the *New York Times* about "the frozen chosen," Chabon discusses his visit to the real Sitka, Alaska, an island that has a very small population of Jews but does have a pie shop in the airport. He also shares that Landsman's dislike of chess derives from his own father teaching him the hated game.

Participating in an interview on the *Washington Post's Book World Live* shortly after the release of *The Yiddish Policemen's Union*, Chabon talks not only about his substantial revisions of that novel but also about the clear separation he makes between a work of fiction and the film adaptation of it. When asked about the preponderance of gay characters in his fiction, he responds by noting the relationship between art and life: since gay people are a part of his life, it makes sense that they find their way into his novels. He also cites the "inverted romanticism and repressed homoeroticism" that exist between men in detective fiction.

Feeling "flattered" when he is compared to such a renowned Jewish writer as Philip Roth, he confirms in the *Washington Post's Book World Live* interview that he thinks of himself as "a Jewish writer" and is "proud to be so identified." Chabon reiterates this pride in his conversation with Sarah Goldstein of *Salon* and suggests an affinity between speculative fiction and Judaism's intense engagement with both history and the futurism of the messianic age. The publication of his Jewish hard-boiled detective novel also was the catalyst for an interview with Gregory Kirschling in *Entertainment Weekly* on his coming out without shame as a lover and writer of genre fiction.

Interviews NPR conducted with Chabon about *The Final Solution* and *Gentlemen of the Road* directly addressed the issue of the perceived literary inferiority of genre fiction. To Steve Inskeep, Chabon expresses his frustration with literary "pigeonholes and categories and labels"; his preferred bookstore would "just have the best 10 percent of everything" in a fiction section. In his interview with Robert Siegel about *Gentlemen of the Road*, Chabon reiterates his view that genre fiction—in this case, an adventure story—does not preclude serious thematics. On the Australian Radio National Book Show, Chabon talked with Ramona Koval about *Gentlemen of the Road* and his desire to integrate Jewish issues into genre fiction. In that segment, he suggests that contemporary Jewish confidence as well as a sense that Jewish security cannot be taken for granted may explain the affinities between *The Yiddish Policemen's Union* and Roth's *The Plot Against America*.

The seder scene in *Wonder Boys* propelled interest in Chabon from the Jewish press. In an interview with Judy Oppenheimer for the *Baltimore Jewish Times* about that novel, Chabon talks about the liberation of writing that scene from a non-Jewish perspective; he also expresses relief that he and his first wife, who was not Jewish, did not have children. For Chabon, raising Jewish children highlights the issue of cultural loss and the fact that parts of Jewish experience verge on extinction. In this conversation with Oppenheimer, Chabon expresses a great deal of self-consciousness about his post-assimilationist desire to "go back now and bridge the breach that was opened up." Chabon reflects upon the loss of Yiddish in this interview published more than a decade before *The Yiddish Policemen's Union*.

Talking with Sandee Brawarsky of *New York Jewish Week* in 1996, Chabon identifies *Wonder Boys* as a book that ended up being Jewish "in a quirky way," although that was not his intention at the outset. In sharp contrast with the previous generation, he finds himself taking for granted the label of "American writer" while needing to "prove" himself as a "Jewish writer." In the interview with *Entertainment Weekly*'s Gregory Kirschling, as well as with Jon Wiener of *Dissent* and *Salon*'s Sarah Goldstein, Chabon voices agreement with his mother's view that questions about and a degree of discomfort with his depiction of Jews have solidified his identity as a Jewish writer. The charges leveled against *The Yiddish Policemen's Union* have him keeping company with Philip Roth, the protypical "bad boy" of Jewish letters.

With Alan Feiler and Abe Novick of the *Baltimore Jewish Times*, Chabon discusses the shift from his youthful alienation from Jewishness to his exploration of it as a source for rootedness. In this interview, he insists that story and character rather than politics motivated his writing of *The Yiddish Policemen's Union*. Reiterating this point, he tells Ben Kaplan of Canada's *National Post*, "If I wanted to send a message, I'd send it Western Union or better, I'd IM." With this reference to instant messaging, Chabon affirms himself as a writer of the Internet generation. Notably, two substantive interviews about Chabon's relationship with Yiddish and its expression in *The Yiddish Policemen's Union*, "The Language Deep, Deep in Chabon's Ear" with Todd Hasak-Lowy and "Arctic Jews" with Jon Wiener, originated on the Web.

The Pulitzer Prize for *The Amazing Adventures of Kavalier and Clay* earned Chabon a spot on *CBS Sunday Morning*'s book series, *In Their Own Words,* with Rita Braver. This television appearance was a profile of his career and his family life. *Kavalier and Clay* has helped to fuel growing interest in the history of comic books and the legendary writers and illustrators that turned the genre into an art form. As a result, Chabon is a talking head in Andrew D. Cooke's documentary *Will Eisner: Portrait of a Sequential Artist* (2007) as well as the History Channel's *Comic Book Superheroes: Unmasked* (2003). In the latter production, available on DVD, Chabon provides commentary on Superman as an immigrant figure as well as the role of comics during World War II. He chronicles his own transition from childhood to adolescence through his shift from the morally unambiguous DC Comics to the more complex Marvel Comics and analyzes the X-Men as metaphors for those who experience themselves as cultural others.

In these media appearances as well as in interviews and book reviews, Michael Chabon is revealed to be the consummate popular literary geek—a rare phenomenon indeed.

DISCUSSION QUESTIONS

- In general, what is the role of reviews in your choice and assessment of novels? How have reviews of Chabon's novels influenced your opinion of his work?
- What questions and information repeatedly appear in interviews with Michael Chabon? To what extent do the type of publication and its target audience determine the content of interviews?
- Several critics suggest that Chabon's female characters are not as well-developed as his male characters. Do you agree with this assessment? Why or why not?

11

WHAT DO I READ NEXT?

Chabon is a diverse writer who crosses all sorts of genre boundaries. These reading recommendations are organized according to some of the qualities and themes in his fiction that may be especially appealing to his readers.

For those who delight in the alternative history aspect of *The Yiddish Policemen's Union*, Philip Roth's *The Plot Against America* (2004), in which the Nazi-sympathizer Charles Lindbergh is elected President of the United States, is a must-read. Most reviews of *Yiddish Policemen* refer to this Roth novel, and it should also be compelling to those interested in the history of anti-Semitism in the United States, an issue in *The Amazing Adventures of Kavalier and Clay*. Philip Dick's *Man in the High Castle* (1962), reissued in a Library of America volume (2007), imagines an America that lost World War II; this novel won the science fiction Hugo Award, as did *The Yiddish Policemen's Union*. Like Chabon, Dick works on the borderlands of genre and literary fiction. Nadine Gordimer's *July's People* (1981) envisions the ending of apartheid in South Africa through violent revolution and charts the shifts in power that occur between a white liberal family and their black servant. Margaret Atwood's *The Handmaid's Tale* (1985) depicts a dystopian world in which theocratic terrorist forces overthrow the U.S. government and install the Republic of Gilead, a totalitarian regime whose overarching mission is the control of women's reproductive lives.

Young men, some of them artists, come of age in Chabon's novels. For those interested in such novels of development, James Joyce's *Portrait of the Artist as a Young Man* (1916), D. H. Lawrence's *Sons and Lovers* (1913), and J. D. Salinger's *Catcher in the Rye* (1951) are classics. Chaim Potok's *My Name Is Asher Lev* (1972) is a fine novel about a young artist striving to negotiate his aesthetic desires and his Judaic commitments. Two of Philip Roth's early novels, *Portnoy's Complaint* (1969) and *Goodbye, Columbus* (1959), are Jewish coming-of-age novels; Chabon cites the latter work, which takes place during the course of a summer, as one of the influences for *The Mysteries of Pittsburgh*. The ways in which a self-involved father fails his sons is a particularly poignant part of Joshua Braff's *The Unthinkable Thoughts of Jacob Green* (2004). Myla Goldberg's coming-of-age novel *Bee Season* (2000) charts a son and daughter's competition for their father's attention.

Gay characters and the blurring of gender and sexual boundaries are an oft-noted feature of Chabon's fiction. Those that find themselves following this strand of Chabon's work might be interested in E. M. Forster's posthumously published *Maurice* (1971), a novel about a young man's sexual awakening in early twentieth-century England; Radclyffe Hall's *The Well of Loneliness* (1928), initially banned in England for its lesbian content; and Rita Mae Brown's *Rubyfruit Jungle* (1973), which counters the tragic narrative of Hall's lesbian classic. David Leavitt's *The Lost Language of Cranes* (1986) is a poetic novel about a young man's coming out process and the new connections he forges with his father. Michael Cunningham's Pulitzer Prize–winning novel *The Hours* (1998) depicts queer love and community as does Cunningham's H*ome at the Edge of the World* (1990); Cunningham's work, like Chabon's, has lent itself to film adaptations.

Chabon's obsession with comics, superheroes, and pop culture is shared by his writer-friend, Jonathan Lethem, whose novel *Fortress of Solitude* (2003) and short story collection *Men and Cartoons* (2004) are companion reads to *The Amazing Adventures of Kavalier and Clay*. Ben Katchor's *Julius Knipl, Real Estate Photographer* (1996), a collection of newspaper comic stories for which Chabon wrote an introduction, pays homage to New York, even if the city of his graphic imagination remains unnamed.

Will Eisner, whose graphic home is also New York, always believed in the artistic value of comics, and Chabon imbues Joe Kavalier with this aesthetic faith. Those who want to learn about the work of Eisner, whom Chabon has called the "father of the graphic novel" and eulogized eloquently in "Thoughts on the Death of Will Eisner," might look at the following works by Eisner: *The Spirit Archives* (2000–); *The Contract with God Trilogy* (2005); *Fagin the Jew* (2003); and *The Plot: The Secret Story of the Protocols of the Elders of Zion* (2005).

Art Spiegelman's classic *Maus: A Survivor's Tale* (1986) resides at the intersection of two of Chabon's interests, the graphic novel and Holocaust representation. Like *Maus*, Thane Rosenbaum's novel *Second Hand Smoke* (1999) details the continuing effects of the Holocaust on the children of survivors. Rosenbaum's *The Golems of Gotham* (2002) imagines survivors as golem figures. Other contemporary fictions that join *Kavalier and Clay* in making use of the golem legend include Cynthia Ozick's *The Puttermesser Papers* (1997), Pete Hamill's *Snow in August* (1997), and Marge Piercy's *He, She, and It* (1991).

The setting of *Kavalier and Clay* shifts from Prague to New York. Jonathan Safran Foer's *Everything Is Illuminated* (2002), Amy Bloom's *Away* (2007), Rebecca Goldstein's *Mazel* (1995), and Dara Horn's *In the Image* (2002) also explore the relationship between Old World and New. Chabon's Jewish characters tend to be cultural Jews, and his depiction of religious life in *The Yiddish Policemen's Union* is limited. Allegra Goodman's *Kaaterskill Falls* (1998) and Tova Mirvis's *The Ladies Auxiliary* (1999) provide complementary depictions of more traditionally observant Jewish Americans.

During the course of *Kavalier and Clay*, Sammy dreams of writing a novel titled *American Disillusionment*, but this ends up becoming an apt description of his life narrative. For those interested in fiction that explores the impossibilities of the American Dream, F. Scott Fitzgerald's *The Great Gatsby* (1925) is a good place to start. Chabon cites that American classic as another influence for *The Mysteries of Pittsburgh*. Philip Roth's *The Human Stain* (2000), which is part academic novel and thus a good companion to *Wonder Boys*, also provides a critical window on American mythologies of the self-made man. E. L. Doctorow's *Ragtime* (1975), Don DeLillo's *Underworld* (1997), and Jennifer Gilmore's *Golden Country* (2006) are novels of historical sweep comparable to *Kavalier and Clay*.

For readers inspired by the adventures of Chabon's wonder boys, whether in the novel of that name or in *Gentlemen of the Road*, Jack Kerouac's classic *On the Road* (1957) is recommended. Those who find themselves drawn to the mystery/detective genre that Chabon calls upon in both *The Final Solution* and *The Yiddish Policemen's Union* might especially like Sir Arthur Conan Doyle's *The Hound of the Baskervilles* (1902), Nicholas Meyer's *The Seven-Per-Cent Solution* (1974), Dashiell Hammett's *The Maltese Falcon* (1930) and *The Thin Man* (1933), as well as Isaac Babel's *The Odessa Stories* reprinted in *The Complete Works of Isaac Babel* (2005). Chabon found much inspiration for *The Yiddish Policemen's Union* in Raymond Chandler's *The Long Goodbye* (1953), an example of genre fiction that he considers a case study of "masculine anxiety" and a great American novel.

RESOURCES

Works by Michael Chabon

The Amazing Adventures of Kavalier and Clay. New York: Random House, 2000.

The Amazing Adventures of the Escapist, Vol. 1. Milwaukie, OR: Dark Horse Comics, 2004.

The Amazing Adventures of the Escapist, Vol. 2. Milwaukie, OR: Dark Horse Comics, 2004.

The Amazing Adventures of the Escapist, Vol. 3. Milwaukie, OR: Dark Horse Comics, 2006.

The Best American Short Stories 2005 (editor), Boston: Houghton Mifflin Harcourt, 2005.

"Breakfast in the Wreck." *Virginia Quarterly Review,* Spring 2004: 33–38.

The Escapists. Milwaukie, OR: Dark Horse Comics, 2007.

The Final Solution. New York: Harper Perennial, 2004.

Gentlemen of the Road. New York: Ballantine, 2007.

Manhood for Amateurs: The Pleasures and Regrets of a Husband, Father, and Son. New York: Harper, 2009. "The Binding of Isaac" and "The Losers' Club" are included in this volume.

Maps and Legends: Reading and Writing along the Borderlands. San Francisco: McSweeney's Books, 2008. "Diving into the Wreck," "Imaginary Homelands," "The Killer Hook," "Maps and Legends," "My Back Pages," "Thoughts on the Death of Will Eisner," and "Trickster in a Suit of Lights" are included in this volume.

McSweeney's Enchanted Chamber of Astonishing Stories (editor). New York: Vintage, 2004.

McSweeney's Mammoth Treasury of Thrilling Tales (editor). New York: Vintage, 2003.

A Model World and Other Stories. New York: HarperCollins, 1991.

The Mysteries of Pittsburgh. New York: Perennial, 1988.

"Obama and the Conquest of Denver." *New York Review of Books,* October 9, 2008.

"The Return of the Amazing Cavalieri." *McSweeney's* 7 (2001): 1–16.

"Revenge of Wolverine." *Harper's,* October 2000, 32–38.

Summerland. New York: Hyperion, 2002.

Werewolves in Their Youth: Stories. New York: Picador, 1999.

Wonder Boys. New York: Picador, 1995.

The Yiddish Policemen's Union. New York: HarperCollins, 2007.

OTHER RESOURCES

Ali, Omer. "Books—Oy Slay!" *Time Out,* June 13, 2007, 54.

Almond, Steve. "These 'Gentlemen' are Swashbucklers, but Little Else." *Boston Globe,* November 17, 2007, C1.

Altschuler, Glenn C. "Two Jewish Gentlemen Hit the Road, Rootless and Restless, in Michael Chabon's *Gentlemen of the Road: A Tale of Adventure.*" *Philadelphia Inquirer,* December 4, 2007.

Bahr, David. "Chabon's Excellent Adventures." *Advocate*, December 9, 2000, 62–63. *Contemporary Literary Criticism,* Gale Literary Databases (accessed May 23, 2009).

Barrie-Anthony, Steven. "The Call of 'D'oh!'" *Los Angeles Times*, November 30, 2005, E1.

Barsanti, Chris. "The Graphic Report . . ." *Kirkus Reviews*, July 13, 2004, 642.

Behlman, Lee. "The Escapist: Fantasy, Folklore and the Pleasures of the Comic in Recent Jewish American Holocaust Fiction." *Shofar: An Interdisciplinary Journal of Jewish Studies* 22, no. 3 (2004): 56–71.

Benfer, Amy. "*The Amazing Adventures of Kavalier and Clay* by Michael Chabon." *Salon,* September 28, 2000. http://www.salon.com/books/review/2000/09/28/chabon/index.html.

Binelli, Mark and Bryce Duffy. "The Amazing Story of the Comic-Book Nerd Who Won the Pulitzer Prize for Fiction." *Rolling Stone,* September, 27, 2001, 58.

Birkerts, Sven. "Fiction in Review." *Yale Review* 84, no. 1 (1996): 157–65. *Contemporary Literary Criticism,* Gale Literary Databases, (accessed June 29, 2008).

Blume, Harvey. "Running Out of Options." *Jerusalem Report,* June 11, 2007, 38.

Book World Live. Interview with Michael Chabon, May 15, 2007. The Washington Post, www.washingtonpost.com. http://www.washingtonpost.com/wp-dyn/content/discussion/2007/05/11/DI2007051101140.html (accessed November 23, 2009).

Braiker, Brian. "That Chabon Sure Has Chutzpah." *Newsweek*, May 7, 2007: 63.

Braver, Rita. "Michael Chabon Makes a Living and Wins the Pulitzer at the Age of 37." *CBS News Sunday Morning*, January 13, 2002. http://www.cbsnews.com/stories/2002/01/09/sunday/main323746.shtml (accessed November 23, 2009).

Brawarsky, Sandee. "Among the Frozen Chosen." *New York Jewish Week*, May 11, 2007, 39.

———. "'Wonder Boy' at the Seder." *New York Jewish Week*, March 29, 1996, 24.

Buchanan, Kyle. "The Geometry of a Pittsburgh Love Story." Advocate.com, January 11, 2008. http://www.advocate.com/Arts_and_Entertainment/Books/The_Geometry_of_a_Pittsburgh_Love_Story/ (accessed November 23, 2009).

Buium, Greg. "Let Him Entertain You." *Globe and Mail* (Canada), June 14, 2008, D14.

Bukiet, Melvin Jules. "Echoes of an Atrocity." *Washington Post*, November 14, 2004, TO7.

Cahill, Bryon. "Michael Chabon: A Writer with Many Faces." *Writing* 27, no.6 (April 2005): 16–19.

Caines, Michael. "The Adventures of Michael Chabon." *Times Literary Supplement* (U.K.), November 28, 2007.

Caldwell, Gail. "The Long Shalom." *Boston Globe*, May 6, 2007, E4.

———. "An Ode to the Golden Age of Comic Book Heroes." *Boston Globe*, November 19, 2000, E1.

Campbell, Frank. "So a Rabbi's Son and an Ethopian Go On This Quest." *Weekend Australian*, December 1, 2007, 12.

Cattan, Nacha. "Kavalier & Clay's Escapist Adventure." *Forward*, December 19, 2003, 10.

Caveney, Graham. "Wonders and Marvels." *Independent* (U.K.), November 4, 2000, 10.

"Chabon's Amazing Rewrite Adventures." *Wall Street Journal*, April 27, 2007, W3.

Chiarella, Tom. "Michael Chabon: 75 Most Influential People of the 21st Century." *Esquire*, September 24, 2008.

Cohen, Patricia. "The Frozen Chosen." *New York Times*, April 29, 2007, 1.

Conan, Neal. "Comic Books." *Talk of the Nation*, NPR, January 9, 2002. http://www.npr.org/templates/story/story.php?storyId=1136016 (accessed November 23, 2009).

Cooke, Andrew D., director. *Will Eisner: Portrait of a Sequential Artist*. DVD. Montilla, 2007.

Cote, Marc. "Under the Glitz, a Literary Hybrid with Profound Understanding." *Globe and Mail* (Canada), July 9, 1988.

Davis, J. Madison. "Mix and Match: Michael Chabon's Imaginative Use of Genre." *World Literature Today*, November/December 2008, 9–11.

Deresiewicz, William. "The Imaginary Jew." *Nation*, May 28, 2007, 44–48.

Dirda, Michael. "The Amazing Adventures of Kavalier and Clay." *Washington Post*, September 17, 2000, X15.

Donahue, Deirdre. "Chabon's Latest Amazing Adventure: Pulitzer for Fiction." *USA Today*, April 19, 2001, 1D.

Dougherty, Robin. "Pow! Zap! It's Wonder Boy." *Boston Globe*, May 13, 2001, L4.

Dunn, Marica. "First-Time Novelist Astounded by Success." *Associated Press*, June 23, 1988. http://www.lexisnexis.com.navigator.southwestern.edu:2048/us/lnacademic/results/docview/docview.do?docLinkInd=true&risb=21_T8141588940&format=GNBFI&sort=RELEVANCE&startDocNo=1&resultsUrlKey=29_T8141588943&cisb=22_T8141588942&treeMax=true&treeWidth=0&csi=304478&docNo=1 (accessed July 9, 2008).

Eder, Richard. "A Bag of Pot, a Purloined Jacket, and Thou." *Los Angeles Times Book Review*, March 26, 1995, 3, 12. *Contemporary Literary Criticism*, Gale Literary Databases (accessed June 30, 2008).

Edwards, Bob. "*The Writing Life*": "Authors Discuss Their Craft in Virtual Roundtable." *Morning Edition*, NPR, July 2, 2003. http://www.npr.org/templates/story/story.php?storyId=1304643 (accessed November 23, 2009).

Ephron, Nora. "You've Got Rapture." *O, the Oprah Magazine*, June 2002.

Eskenazi, Joe. "On the Same Page: Michael Chabon, Ayelet Waldman Write Together—Separately—in Berkeley." *Jewish News Weekly of Northern California*, September 20, 2007, 26–27.

Feiler, Alan H. and Abe Novick. "Inside Passage: Michael Chabon's Jewish Journey Leads to a Fictional Alaska." *Baltimore Jewish Times*, June 22, 2007, 47–48.

Flagg, Gordon. "*The Amazing Adventures of the Escapist, Vol.1.*" *Booklist*, August 1, 2004.

Franklin, Ruth. "God's Frozen People." *Slate*, May 8, 2007. http://www.slate.com/id/2165763/.

Freedman, Samuel G. "Chabon's Choice." *Jerusalem Post*, July 13, 2007, 4.

Friedell, Deborah. "Bird of the Baskervilles." *New York Times*, November 14, 2004, 57.

Furst, Joshua. "A Long Way from Zion: Michael Chabon's Yiddish Noir." *Zeek*, July 2007.

"Gaseous 'Clay': An Online Guide to Deciphering Michael Chabon's Comic Marvel." EW.com, April 19, 2002. http://www.ew.com/ew/article/0,,250753,00.html (accessed November 23, 2009).

Giles, Jeff. "He's a Real Boy Wonder." *Newsweek*, April 10, 1995, 76.

Gleiberman, Owen. "The Mysteries of Pittsburgh." *Entertainment Weekly*, April 11, 2009, 47.

Goldstein, Sarah. "Jews on Ice." *Salon*, May 4, 2007. http://www.salon.com/books/int/2007/05/04/chabon/index.html (accessed November 23, 2009).

Gorra, Michael. "Youth and Consequences." *New Republic*, June 26. 1995, 40–41. *Contemporary Literary Criticism*, Gale Literary Databases (accessed June 29, 2008).

Gross, Terry. "From Michael Chabon, Noir and Niftorim in the North," *Fresh Air*, National Public Radio, May 3, 2007. http://www.npr.org/templates/story/story.php?storyId=9974891 (accessed November 23, 2009).

———. "Writer Michael Chabon," (discussing *The Amazing Adventures of Kavalier and Clay) Fresh Air*, NPR, May 1, 2001. http://www.npr.org/templates/story/story.php?storyId=1122285 (accessed November 23, 2009).

Grossman, Lev. "The Genius Who Wanted to Be a Hack." *Time*, November 15, 2007, 74.

———. "Pop Goes the Literature." *Time*, December 13, 2004, 71.

Hansen, Liane. "*Wonder Boys* Chronicles Fictional Writer of Fiction." *Weekend Edition*, NPR, May 28, 1995. http://www.npr.org/templates/story/story.php?storyId=1005665 (accessed November 23, 2009).

Hanson, Curtis, director. *Wonder Boys*. DVD. Paramount, 2000.

Harris, Ben. "Oy Brother: Coens to Take On Michael Chabon Best-Seller." *Jewish News Weekly of Northern California*, February 29, 2008, 4B.

Harris, Mark. "Road Warriors." *Entertainment Weekly*, November 2, 2007, 68.

Hasak-Lowy, Todd. "The Language Deep, Deep in Chabon's Ear." JBooks, December 17, 2008. http://www.jbooks.com/interviews/index/IP_Hasak Lowy_Chabon.htm (accessed November 23, 2009).

Henderson, Eleanor. "From Pittsburgh to Sitka." *Virginia Quarterly Review*, Summer 2007, 248–257.

Hensher, Philip. "Busy Going Nowhere." *Guardian*, May 19, 1995, T7.

Horspool, David. "Sam and Joe Take On the Nazis." *Times Literary Supplement* (U.K.), October 6, 2000, 24. *Contemporary Literary Criticism*, Gale Literary Databases (accessed May 23, 2009).

Houpt, Simon. "An Author Who Has Finally Found His Home." *Globe and Mail* (Canada), May 19, 2007, R17.

Hubbard, Kim and Anne-Marie Otey. "Natural Wonder." *People*, June 26, 1995, 63.

Inskeep, Steve. "Pulitzer Prize Winner Revives Sherlock Holmes." *Morning Edition*, NPR, December 20, 2004. http://www.npr.org/templates/story/story.php?storyId=4235933 (accessed November 23, 2009).

"Is Michael Chabon's New Book Anti-Semitic?" Gawker, April 22, 2007. http://gawker.com/254341/is-michael-chabons-new-book-anti+semitic (accessed November 23, 2009).

"IT Script." *Entertainment Weekly*, June 28, 2002, 44.

Jeffries, Stuart. "The Language of Exile." *Guardian*, June 7, 2007, 12.

Jelbert, Steve. "Books: *The Amazing Adventures of Kavalier and Clay*." *Times* (U.K.), July 28 2001, 21.

Jonas, Gerald. "It's a Bird, It's a Plane, It's an Angry Jew! A Comic Artist's Revenge Fantasies Animate a 20th-Century Epic: *The Amazing Adventures of Kavalier & Clay*." *Forward*, February 2, 2001, 13.

Kahn, Joseph. "Writer's Balk." *Boston Globe*, May 22, 1995, 30.

Kakutani, Michiko. "A Novel about a Novelist and His Messy Life." *New York Times*, March 17, 1995, 28.

Kalfus, Ken. "The Golem Knows." *New York Times Book Review*, September 24, 2000, 8.

Kamine, Mark. "Chasing His Bliss." *New York Times*, June 29, 2008, 21.

Kaplan, Ben. "From Domestic Life to a World of Adventure." *National Post* (Canada), November 8, 2007, B6.

———. "Politics Can't Spoil This Wild Imagination." *National Post* (Canada), May 24, 2007, AL12.

Kaveney, Roz. "Panic in Pittsburgh." *New Statesman and Society*, June 9, 1995, 38. *Contemporary Literary Criticism*, Gale Literary Databases (accessed June 30, 2008).

Kelly, Stuart. "*Gentlemen of the Road*: Roaming Rogues in a Serial Thriller." *Scotland on Sunday*, November 25, 2007, 12.

Kirschling, Gregory. "The New Adventures of Michael Chabon." *Entertainment Weekly*, May 11, 2007, 46–48.

Klein, Julia. "On the Heels of One Literary Success, a Young Author Is Shocked by Another." *Philadelphia Inquirer*, April 19, 1995, E01.

Koval, Ramona. "Michael Chabon: Swashbuckling Gentleman of the Road." *The Book Show*, ABC Radio National (Australia), August 5, 2008, http://www.abc.net.au/rn/bookshow/stories/2008/2321579.htm (accessed November 23, 2009).

Kroopnick, Steve, director. *Comic Book Superheroes Unmasked*. DVD. A&E, 2003.

Lambert, Josh. "Chabon Returns, Still Crusading for Fun in Literature; 'The Final Solution: A Story of Detection.'" *Forward*, October 29, 2004, 13.

Leopold, Todd. "A Mystery with an 'If Only' Twist on History." CNN.com, June 28, 2007. http://www.cnn.com/2007/SHOWBIZ/books/06/28/michael.chabon/index.html (accessed November 23, 2009).

Levi, Jonathan. "Hope against Hope." *Los Angeles Times Book Review*, October 8, 2000, 2. *Contemporary Literary Criticism*, Gale Literary Databases (accessed May 23, 2009).

Lotozo, Eils. "*The Amazing Adventures of Kavalier and Clay* by Michael Chabon." *Philadelphia Inquirer*, October 5, 2000.

Maslin, Janet. "A Life and Death Story Set in Comic Book Land." *New York Times*, September 21, 2000, 10.

McDermott, Alice. "Gangsters and Pranksters." *New York Times Book Review*, April 3, 1988, 7.

McKay, Ron. "How to Make New Readers Start Here." *Campaign*, June 3, 1988.

Miller, Laura. "The Lost Adventure of Childhood." *Salon*, October 22, 2002. http://www.salon.com/books/int/2002/10/22/chabon/ (accessed November 23, 2009).

Moore, Dennis. "*Gentlemen of the Road* Walks on the Wild Side." *USA Today*, November 21, 2007, 06D.

Ogle, Connie. "Yiddish Detective Tracks a Killer." *Miami Herald*, May 7, 2007.

"Oh, Brothers!" *Baltimore Jewish Times*, February 22, 2008, 6.

Oppenheimer, Judy. "Pop Fiction: Novelist Nouvelle (and New Dad) Michael Chabon Is Lovin'Life." *Baltimore Jewish Times*, August 11, 1995, 46.

Oppenheimer, Mark. "Jewish Noir." *Forward*, April 20, 2007, B1–B2.

Passaro, Vince. "This Is an Exodus?" *O, the Oprah Magazine*, May 2007.

Perle, Liz. "Alternate Reality." *Publishers Weekly*, September 24, 2007, 31.

Phillips, Julie. "In Conversation ... With Michael Chabon." *Washington Post*, November 4, 2007, BW09.

———. "Michael Chabon and Daniel Mendelsohn in Amsterdam." *Critical Mass*, February 13, 2008. http://bookcritics.org/blog/archive/Guest_Post_Michael_Chabon_Daniel_Mendelsohn_in_Amsterdam/ (accessed January 8, 2009).

Pinsker, Sanford. "Northern Exposure: Imagining Yiddishland in Alaska." *New Jersey Jewish News*, June 14, 2007, 38.

———. "Wonder Boys." *Jewish Exponent*, July 28, 1995, 7X.

Podhoretz, John. "Escapists." *Commentary*, June 2001, 68.

Pols, Mary F. "Chabon Celebrates as 'Kavalier and Clay' Picks Up a Pulitzer." *Contra Costa Times*, April 17, 2001.

"Questions for Michael Chabon." *New York Times Magazine*, February 8, 2007.

Rafferty, Terence. "Cops and Rabbis." *New York Times*, May 13, 2007, 10.

Rengger, Patrick. "Chabon's Newest Not Wonderful." *Financial Post*, March 2, 1996, 22.

Schifrin, Daniel. "Solving Jewish History." *New York Jewish Week*, June 29, 2007, 50.

Scott, A. O. "A Stockbroker in Training Has Turns in His Journey." *New York Times*, April 10, 2009.

Sedgwick, Eve Kosofsky. *Between Men: English Literature and Male Homosocial Desire*. New York: Columbia University Press, 1985.

See, Lisa. "Michael Chabon: Wonder Boy in Transition." *Publishers Weekly*, April 10, 1995, 44–45. *Contemporary Literary Criticism*, Gale Literary Databases (accessed June 30, 2008).

Shandler, Jeffrey. "Imagining Yiddishland: Language, Place and Memory." *History and Memory* 15, no.1 (2003): 123–149.

Siegel, Robert. "Chabon's Latest Is Literary, Linguistic Adventure." *All Things Considered*, NPR, October 30, 2007. http://www.npr.org/templates/story/ story.php?storyId=15773943 (accessed November 23, 2009).

Simeone, Lisa. "Author Michael Chabon." *All Things Considered*, NPR, May 6, 2001. http://www.npr.org/templates/story/story.php?storyId=1122517 (accessed November 23, 2009).

Smith, Kyle. "Novelist's Ugly View of Jews." *New York Post*, April 22, 2007.

Sommer, Allison Kaplan. "The Adventures of Chabon and Waldman." *Moment*, August 31, 2001, 28.

Spanberg, Erik. "Able to Leap over Literary Barriers in a Single Book." *Christian Science Monitor*, November 30, 2004, 17.

Sragow, Michael. "Wonderful Movie." *Salon*, November 10, 2000. http:// www.salon.com/ent/movies/feature/2000/11/10/wonder_boys/index.html (accessed November 23, 2009).

Streitfeld, David. "Book Report." *Washington Post*, February 28, 1999, 13.

———. "Cyberstrokes." *Washington Post*, June 9, 1995, B01.

———. "Young Writers at Work." *Washington Post*, February 21, 1988, X15.

Tandon, Bharat. "A Novelist's Nightmare." *Times Literary Supplement*, April 21, 1995, 20. *Contemporary Literary Criticism*, Gale Literary Databases (accessed June 30, 2008).

Tayler, Christopher. "Young Blades for Hire." *Guardian*, November 3, 2007.

Teitelbaum, Sheli. "Men in Tights." *Jerusalem Report*, January 1, 2001, 47.

Thurber, Rawson Marshall, director. *The Mysteries of Pittsburgh*. DVD. Arclight Films, 2008.

Tobias, Scott. "Michael Chabon."*Onion A.V. Club*, November 22, 2000. http:// www.avclub.com/articles/michael-chabon,13688/ (accessed December 12, 2009).

Travers, Peter. "Movies: *Wonder Boys*." *Rolling Stone*, March 16, 2000, 81.

Troy, Gil. "Group Pride Guarantees Individual Freedom." *Jerusalem Post*, June 30, 2008, 13.

Vail, Kathleen. "Literature or Threat: Authors Support Student Writer." *American School Board Journal*, January 2004, 5.

Vandermeer, Jeff. "Read Michael Chabon's Script for 'Spider-Man 2.'" io9.com. http://io9.com/379291/read-michael-chabons-script-for-spider+ man-2 (accessed November 23, 2009).

Waldman, Ayelet. *Bad Mother: A Chronicle of Maternal Crimes, Minor Calamities, and Occasional Moments of Grace*. New York: Doubleday, 2009.

———. "Living Out Loud—Online." *Salon*, March 14, 2005. http://www. salon.com/mwt/col/waldman/2005/03/14/blog/ (accessed November 23, 2009).

———. "Truly, Madly, Guiltily." *New York Times*, March 27, 2005.

————. "'You're Supposed to Marry the Person You Love, Mom.'" *Salon*, March 28, 2005. http://dir.salon.com/story/mwt/col/waldman/2005/03/28/gay_marriage/index.html (accessed November 23, 2009).

Wall, Alexandra J. "Married Writers to Discuss Craft at CCJCC Book Fest." *Jewish Bulletin of Northern California*, November 10, 2000, 31A.

Wiener, Jon. "Arctic Jews: An Interview with Michael Chabon." *Dissent*, April 14, 2007. http://www.dissentmagazine.org/online.php?id=10 (accessed November 23, 2009).

Wilson, Craig. "Chabon's Next Chapter." *USA Today*, March 30, 1995, 1D.

Wisse, Ruth R. "Slap Shtick." *Commentary*, July 2007, 73–77.

Yanofsky, Joel. "Eclectic Essays." *Gazette* (Montreal), May 17, 2008, 17.

————. "The Land of 'the Frozen Chosen.'" *Gazette* (Montreal), May 5, 2007, J5.

Yardley, Jonathan. "The Paper Chase." *Washington Post Book World*, March 19, 1995, 3. *Contemporary Literary Criticism*, Gale Literary Databases (accessed June 30, 2008).

Ybarra, Michael J. "The Novelist as Wonder Boy." *Los Angeles Times*, October 9, 2000, E1, E4. *Contemporary Literary Criticism*, Gale Literary Databases (accessed June 29, 2008).

Zipp, Yvonne. "Two 'Gentlemen of the Road.'" *Christian Science Monitor*, November 6, 2007, 13.

INDEX

abortion, 7–8, 18, 53, 58, 59, 70, 74

adventure fiction: and Chabon's works generally, 11; *Gentlemen of the Road* as, 6, 18–19, 86, 99, 103

"Adventure of the Empty House, The" (Conan Doyle), 85

"Adventure of the Final Problem, The" (Conan Doyle), 5, 16, 85

Advocate, 73, 98

Albert Vetch, aka August Van Zorn (character), 29, 30, 34–35, 37, 84

alcohol abuse. *See* substance abuse

Aleykhem, Sholem, 66

Almond, Steve, 99

Alter Klayman, aka Mighty Molecule and Professor Alphonse von Clay (character), 47

Alter Litvak (character), 57–59, 62, 65, 66

alternative history: in *Gentlemen of the Road,* 6, 18–19; novels using, 105; in *The Yiddish Policemen's Union,* 5–6, 9, 17–18, 53–59, 66–67, 75–76, 105. *See also* historical novels

Amanda Leer (character), 32

Amazing Adventures of Kavalier and Clay, The (Chabon): anti-Semitism in, 14, 16, 41, 47–48, 49, 50, 105; and Chabon's love for popular culture and genre fiction, 84–85; characters of, 44–50; and comics, 3–4, 14–16, 39–44, 47, 51, 72, 77, 81–82, 85, 95, 97–98, 100; as coming-of-age narrative, 11, 15–16; comparable and complementary works to, by other writers, 106, 107; critical response to, 1, 4, 83, 97–98; Czech fan film adaptation of, 93; discussion questions on, 51; father-son relationship in, 50–51, 70, 71; film adaptation of, 1, 78–79, 92; golem legend in, 4, 14–15, 40, 44, 46–47, 82, 98; historical consciousness in, 9, 14–16; Holocaust in, 14, 39–41, 50, 71, 75, 76, 86; influences on, 3–4; isolation of male character in, 73–74; Jewish themes in, 4, 14–16, 39–41, 50, 71, 74–76, 98; male-male relationships and gay characters in, 15, 42, 43, 48–49, 51, 71, 72–73, 98; plot summary of, 39–44; Pulitzer Prize for, 1, 4, 39, 98, 100, 104; research for, 4; Sammy's dream of writing novel in, 107; Senate subcommittee hearings in, 44, 72, 82; setting of, as shifting from Prague to New York, 107; themes of, 50–51; violence in, 74–75; writing of, 101

About the Author

HELENE MEYERS, Professor of English and McManis University Chair at Southwestern University, is the author of *Femicidal Fears: Narratives of the Female Gothic Experience* (SUNY, 2001). She is writing a book on narratives of Jewish identity in contemporary literature; articles related to that project have appeared in *Shofar* and *Tulsa Studies in Women's Literature*.